STUDIES IN HISTORY, ECONOMICS AND PUBLIC LAW

Edited by the

FACULTY OF POLITICAL SCIENCE
OF COLUMBIA UNIVERSITY

---

NUMBER 354

# THE LARGE ESTATES OF BYZANTINE EGYPT

BY

EDWARD ROCHIE HARDY, JR.

## FRONTISPIECE

The consular diptych of Apion II, reproduced opposite, is preserved in the cathedral of Oviedo.[1] The inscription is:

V(ir) INL(ustris) COM(es) DEVV (otissimorum) DOMM(esticorum) ET CONS(ul) OR(dinarius)

FL(avius) STRATEGIUS APION STRATEGIUS APION

[1] Description in Richard Delbrueck, *Die Consulardiptychen und verwandte Denkmäler* (Richard Delbrueck and Hans Lietzmann, *Studien zur Spätantiken Kunstgeschichte*, 2), Berlin, 1929, 2 vols., vol. i, pp. 150-151; plate in vol. ii, no. 33.

# THE LARGE ESTATES OF BYZANTINE EGYPT

BY

EDWARD ROCHIE HARDY, Jr., Ph.D.

*Fellow and Tutor, General Theological Seminary*
*New York*

NEW YORK
COLUMBIA UNIVERSITY PRESS
London: P. S. King & Son, Ltd.
1931

PRINTED IN THE UNITED STATES OF AMERICA

Memoriae matris optimae sacrum

ACKNOWLEDGMENTS

My deepest thanks are due to Professor W. L. Westermann, under whose direction this study has been written, and to Mr. H. I. Bell, now Keeper of Manuscripts at the British Museum, whom I have had the privilege of consulting throughout. In addition, I am obligated to conversations with Professor Ulrich Wilcken of Berlin and Professor A. S. Hunt of Oxford, Professor M. Rostovtzeff of Yale, and Professor Austin P. Evans and Assistant Professor A. Arthur Schiller of Columbia. Professor Gregor Zereteli of Tiflis very kindly sent me a copy of his publication of Russian and Georgian papyri and the Very Rev. Macimiliano Arboleya-Martinez, Dean of Oviedo, a photograph of the consular diptych which is used for the frontispiece.

General Seminary, New York,
March, 1931.

# TABLE OF CONTENTS

## CHAPTER III

### Other Proprietors of the Period



## CHAPTER IV

### Feudalism and Serfdom

## CHAPTER V

### Estate Management

## CHAPTER VI

### The Estates in the Social and Economic Life of Egypt

## CHAPTER VII

### Epilogue

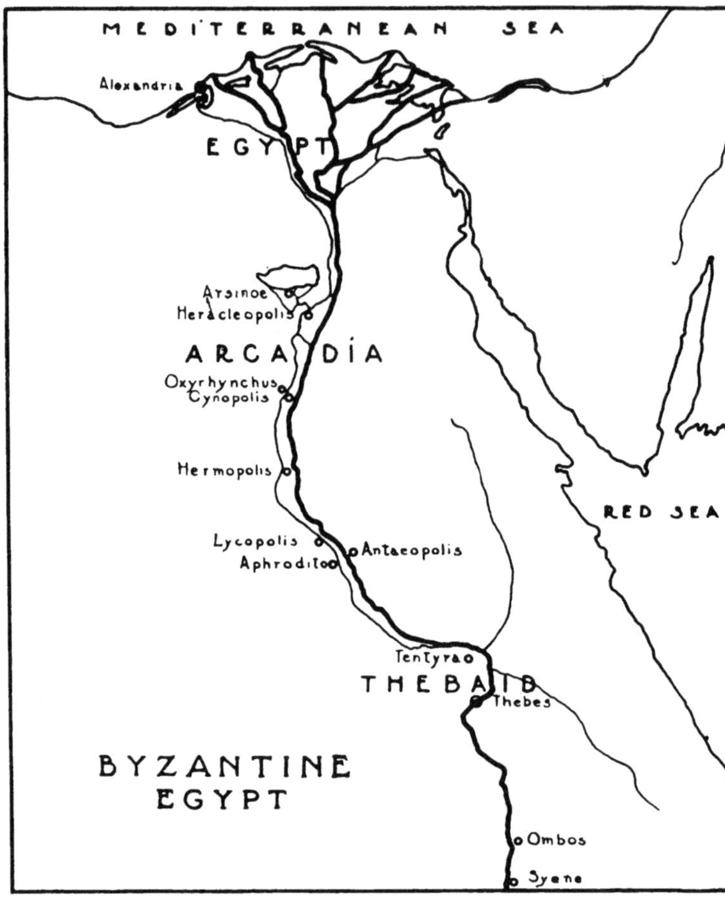
MEDITERRANEAN SEA
Alexandria
EGYPT
Arsinoe
Heracleopolis
ARCADIA
Oxyrhynchus
Cynopolis
Hermopolis
Lycopolis
Antaeopolis
Aphrodito
Tentyra
THEBAID
Thebes
RED SEA
BYZANTINE
EGYPT
Ombos
Syene

# CHAPTER I

## BYZANTINE EGYPT

EGYPT was never a typical Roman province. In its Byzantine period, however, it gives us our one chance to look intimately into the life of a section of the later Roman empire. It was a section, moreover, in which the tendencies of the period were not complicated by extensive foreign influence or barbarian invasion. The natural desire to discover the background of the Mohammedan conquest which was so suddenly to deprive the empire of its non-Greek provinces adds to the interest of Byzantine Egyptian history.

The old and new evidence on Byzantine Egypt has been worked up in a series of brilliant monographs. In 1909 Gelzer sketched the history of the political divisions of Egypt and outlined the social development in its interaction with the political.[1] Three years later Jean Maspero collected our information on the military organization of the period,[2] and at his untimely death left nearly complete the manuscript of a work on its ecclesiastical history, since edited by Fortescue and Wiet.[3] The accumulation of material continued, and

[1] Matthias Gelzer, *Studien zur byzantinischen Verwaltung Aegyptens* in *Leipziger Historische Abhandlungen*, vol. xiii, Leipzig, 1909.

[2] Jean Maspero, *Organization militaire de l'Égypte byzantine* in *Bibliothèque de l'école des hautes études, sciences historiques et philologiques*, fasc. 201, Paris, 1912.

[3] Jean Maspero, *Histoire des patriarches d'Alexandrie* in *Bibliothèque de l'école des hautes études, sciences historiques et philologiques*, fasc. 237, Paris, 1923.

the civil administration which Gelzer had studied in outline has now been systematically described by Rouillard.[1]

From these studies and the other work which has been done, it has become apparent that the sixth century forms a distinct period in Egyptian history, differing alike in spirit and in organization from the fourth and the preceding Roman centuries. The term Byzantine Egypt will, therefore be used in the present study for this period whose boundaries are the Mohammedan conquest of 640 on one side and the end of the fifth century on the other. The Arab conquest obviously put an end to Byzantine Egypt, while the obscurity of the fifth century divides the culture, which preceeded it from that which followed.

In Byzantine Egypt we see a mixture of at least three different cultures. We may illustrate these from the career of the notary Dioscorus, whose papers form a large part of the sixth-century papyri from Aphrodito. The Greco-Roman tradition was by no means dead. Dioscorus in his village in upper Egypt was writing poetic eulogies which he seems to have thought were in a classical style, and which were at least full of mythological references.[2] His active life was lived in frequent contact with the turbulent government of the Egypt of his day. In his business affairs he was in touch with factors which in the West were beginning the formation of the middle ages. Egyptian national life was reviving with great vigor after centuries of foreign rule; and Dioscorus, for all his Greek culture, obviously thought in Coptic.[3]

[1] Germaine Rouillard, *L'administration civile de l'Égypte byzantine*, 2nd ed., Paris, 1928.

[2] On Dioscorus see Jean Maspero, "Un dernier poète grec d'Égypte, Dioscore, fils d'Apollos" in *Revue des études grecques*, vol. xxiv, 1911, pp. 426-481.

[3] *Cf.* his glossary of Greek words into Coptic, H. I. Bell and W. E. Crum, "A Greek-Coptic Glossary" in *Aegyptus*, vol. vi, 1925, pp. 177-226.

It is easy to write of the period in a somewhat dramatic manner. The mediaeval analogies which genuinely exist in many of its features are sometimes over-stressed. Thus a recent article speaks of the great lords of Byzantine Egypt as paying the government a lump sum, so that they were rather tributaries than agents in collecting its taxes, and adds:

Thus by the end of the sixth century there was not much of Egypt left under the effective rule of the emperor; the country was parcelled out into semi-independent estates, somewhat resembling the feudal lordships of mediaeval Europe, interspersed with large areas controlled by religious corporations.[1]

The present study aims mainly to collect material on which may be based a judgment as to the nature of these estates. It will proceed chiefly by describing their operation. The richest material for this comes from the property of the Apion family, but the Apion papyri are well supplemented from other estates.

The rarity of fifth-century papyri makes it hard to see just how the government and social organization of Byzantine Egypt came into being. In many cases we see new forms developing in the fourth century, and then we are left to conjecture as to how they led to the results which appear in the sixth.[2] The gradual revision of the political divisions is one of the few exceptions. We can trace it step by step until the Diocletianic system of provinces and separation of civil and military power was finally abolished by an edict of Justinian,

[1] J. G. Milne, "Egyptian Nationalism under Greek and Roman Rule" in *The Journal of Egyptian Archaeology*, vol. xiv, 1928, pp. 226-234, p. 233.

[2] *Cf.* L. Mitteis and U. Wilcken, *Grundzüge und Chrestomathie der Papyruskunde*, Leipzig, 1912, 4 vols., vol. i, chap. 7, and H. I. Bell, "An Epoch in the Agrarian History of Egypt" in *Recueil d'études égyptologiques dédiées à la mémoire de Jean-Francois Champollion, Bibliothèque de l'école des hautes études, sciences historiques et philologiques*, fasc. 234, Paris, 1922, pp. 261-271.

issued in 538 after a period of disorder unusual even for Alexandria.[1]

The frame of government established by this edict continued for the remainder of the Roman period. Egypt, with Libya, was still unofficially spoken of as constituting a " diocese," [2] but its only political unity lay in the centralization of taxes at Alexandria for transmission to Constantinople.[3] The ancient title of prefect of Egypt had given way to the new phrase " augustal duke," and the governor at Alexandria now had as equals the governors of four provinces,—Augustamnica in the eastern Delta, Arcadia, named after the emperor Arcadius, in central Egypt, the Thebaid, and Libya. At the head of each province stood a governor with civil and military power.[4] The *praesides,* coordinate civil governors in the fourth century, were now subordinate officials under these dukes.[5] The equality and mutual independence of the provinces were probably responsible for the catastrophic lack of cooperation which weakened the resistance to the Moslem armies.[6]

For purposes of local government the old nomes had, practically speaking, come into being again under the name of pagarchies. The civil administration in each was headed by a pagarch, although the metropolis was perhaps theoretically not under his jurisdiction.[7] At his side was the tribune in

[1] Edict xiii, *Corpus Juris Civilis,* vol. iii, Novellae, ed. R. Schoell and W. Kroll, 4th ed., 1912; Gelzer, *op. cit.,* pp. 2-36; Rouillard, *op. cit.,* pp. 16-25. Gelzer and Rouillard discuss the date. For the reason for giving it as 538 rather than 538-9, see *infra,* p. 31.

[2] Maspero, *Organization militaire,* pp. 7-10.

[3] Edict xiii, 4.

[4] Rouillard, *op. cit.,* pp. 27-47; Gelzer, *op. cit.,* pp. 21-31.

[5] Rouillard, *op. cit.,* pp. 47-52.

[6] See A. J. Butler, *The Arab Conquest of Egypt and the last thirty years of the Roman dominion,* Oxford, 1902. This must now be read in the light of Maspero's *Organization militaire.*

[7] Rouillard, *op. cit.,* pp. 52-62. Some support for the theory that the

command of the military forces, consisting of one or more *numeri*.[1]

Justinian's edict frankly admits that the first concern of the augustal duke at Alexandria was to see that the embolé ("happy shipment," αἰσία ἐμβολή) was collected and sent on.[2] In this grain tax for the feeding of Constantinople we recognize under a new name the institution which had been Rome's chief interest in Egypt since the days of Augustus. The amount expected from the whole of Egypt was eight million artabae.[3] A money tax known as naulage (ναῦλον) was collected at the same time to pay for the shipment of the grain.[4]

There is still some uncertainty as to how many money taxes were collected in our period. Theoretically the revenues assigned to the treasury of the praetorian prefect were collected by his agents in Egypt, those belonging to the Count of the Sacred Largesses by the dukes and their subordinates.[5] The money tax on land, however, usually appears in our documents as if it were a single item, payable through a single office.[6] We must assume that the theoretical system was simplified in practice. It is possible that some kind of fusion took place; this is perhaps confirmed by the way in which the officials called *scriniarii* appear in our documents. In the edict of 538 they are mentioned as subordinates of the Praetorian Prefect whom the local authorities must assist, by force if necessary, but are not to interfere with; in papyri

metropolis still controlled an independent tax collecting unit may be found in P. Cairo, 67009, 20: "the unfortunate city and its περιπρακτορία."

[1] Maspero, *Organization militaire*, pp. 88-99.

[2] Edict xiii, 4.

[3] Edict xiii, 7; see discussion in Rouillard, *op. cit.*, pp. 124-126.

[4] Edict xiii, 7-8; Rouillard, *op. cit.*, pp. 143-148.

[5] Edict xiii, 9-11.

[6] *E. g.*, P. Ox. 197-198.

they are members of the ducal staff.[1] There are a few references, especially in cities, to the two kinds of taxes,[2] but the distinction does not seem even there to have been important. The principal charges collected in addition to the land tax were the poll tax (διαγραφή) and the perequisites of officials (συνήθειαι). The latter were developing from merely customary payments into an additional tax for the support of the provincial government.[3]

Municipal government still continued to exist. The most important local officials in the old nome capitals were now the defensors, who presided over the senate, and exercised various administrative functions. The office was held as a liturgy (i.e., a public function performed as a charge on one's property) for a two-year term by local notables.[4] The normal village organization reproduced on a smaller scale that of the cities. A body of *protocometae* (πρωτοκωμῆται, first men of the village) took the place of the senate, and further officials were employed as the size and conditions of the villarge might require.[5] Judicial authority was mainly in the hands of the defensors, the pagarchs, and the higher governors.[6] Police duties were performed by various kinds of guards and watchmen, often headed by officials called *riparii*. The dignity of the latter naturally varied, since they might be *riparii* of larger or smaller places.[7]

[1] Edict xiii, 9-11; Rouillard, *op. cit.*, pp. 93-94.

[2] *E. g.*, *largitionalia* in P. Stud. Pal. xx, 143 (C. Wesseley, *Studien zur Palaeographie und Papyruskunde*, vol. xx, Leipzig, 1921). *Arcarica*, for the *arca* of the Praetorian Prefect, in P. Ox. 2020 (Bernard P. Grenfell, Arthur S. Hunt, H. I. Bell, *The Oxyrhynchus Papyri*, London, Egypt Exploration Fund, 17 vols., 1898-1927).

[3] Rouillard, *op. cit.*, pp. 76-81.

[4] *Ibid.*, 62-67.

[5] Rouillard *op. cit.*, pp. 67-74; P. Ox. 1835, note to line 2.

[6] Rouillard, *op. cit.*, pp. 149-162.

[7] *Ibid.*, pp. 163-166.

Changes in the life of the people accompanied the political reorganization of Byzantine Egypt. Egyptian national feeling was reviving,[1] and the Coptic church had become its organ.[5] After 451 the Copts were separated from Greek Christendom under color of monophysite belief. It is significant, as indicating the national and anti-imperial character of the Coptic church, that the orthodox body was referred to, from the Syriac word for king, as Melkite, i.e., imperialist. On the whole, the national church was fairly successful in maintaining itself in our period. Not until 537 was a Melkite patriarch established at Alexandria.[2] Not until 630, when the defection of the Copts during the Persian invasion had roused the government, was any systematic attempt actually made to stamp out their organization all over Egypt.[3] Meanwhile the Coptic language and literature were gradually replacing Greek culture throughout the country. The attitude of the people at large towards the Roman government was one of apathy, if not quite of open hostility. It would indeed have been surprising if the people of Egypt had felt any great enthusiasm for a government which demanded so much and gave so little.[4] The language of Justinian's edict of reorganization, with its concencentration of interest on the exploitation of the country, is typical of the Roman attitude. The Egyptian reaction is understandable; it is in fact remarkable that it was not more violent and did not affect Byzantine government as well as Byzantine culture.

Meanwhile Egypt was sharing, although perhaps with

[1] Maspero, *Histoire*, pp. 23-27; Rouillard, *op. cit.*, pp. 186 *et seq.*

[2] *Ibid.*, pp. 135-138.

[3] Butler, *op. cit.*, pp. 168-193.

[4] *Cf.* the collection of evidence on this point in Leopold Wenger, *Volk und Staat in Ägypten am Ausgang der Römerherrschaft*, Munich, 1922, 58 pp.

some distinctive features, the social developments which were taking place throughout the empire. The depression of the municipal aristocracy on which the early empire depended was reflected in the very creation of the pagarchies, which deprived the municipal senates of most of their administrative functions; though it must be remarked that the municipal notables still meet us as landowners in the sixth century. The twin institutions of the colonate and patronage laid the foundations of a new agrarian system. The binding of the peasant to the soil was no novelty in Egypt. It was the substitution of private landowners for the state as the beneficaries of this binding which made it the basis of a semi-feudal order.[1]

Patronage meets us in Egypt from the fourth century on. From the point of view of the government it was a conspiracy between the peasants and their patrons to evade the payment of taxes.[2] The development of patronage reflected, in two distinct ways, abuses which existed in the government. The oppression of tax collectors drove peasants to seek the protection of patrons,[3] and these patrons themselves were often high officials, civil or military, taking advantage of their position.[4]

A series of laws against patronage remained unenforced.[5] Finally the government realized that it was more important to collect its revenue than to collect it from any particular

[1] M. Rostowzew, *Studien zur Geschichte des römischen Kolonats* (*Archiv für Papyrusforschung*, Beiheft 1), Leipzig, 1910, p. 227.

[2] The development is traced, mainly from the legal sources, in F. de Zulueta, *Patronage in the Later Empire* (in Paul Vinogradoff, *Oxford Studies in Social and Legal History*, vol. i, 2), Oxford, 1909.

[3] *Cf.* Gelzer, *op. cit.*, pp. 81-83.

[4] *Cf.* the list of patrons in the laws as analyzed in de Zulueta, *op. cit.*, pp. 6-14.

[5] C. T. xi, 24 (*Theodosiani Libri xvi*, ed. Th. Mommsen, Berlin, 1905, 2 vols.).

set of people. In 415 it capitulated, at least as far as Egypt was concerned, by recognizing patrons as proprietors. The central provisions in the law by which this was done are worth quoting in full:

Let the investigation of Valerius, Theodore, and Tharsacius cease, provided only that those who have begun since the consulship of Caesarius and Atticus [397 A. D.] to hold their lands under patronage are to be arraigned under judgment of the augustal prefect; we wish them to perform all their duties to the state, so that the name of patron may be entirely abolished. But lands which were established in their present condition previously are to be retained by their former holders, if they in accordance with the old census clearly acknowledge in due proportion their duties to the state and obligation to provide liturgists, as the homologi coloni are known to provide them.[1]

Although some details are obscure, the general meaning is quite clear. The year 397 is fixed as the limit of legal memory for cases against patronage.[2] The next clause in the law attempted to guarantee the integrity of *metrocomiae* [3] by pro-

[1] C. T. xi, 24, 6 pr. Valerii, Theodori et Tharsacii examinatio conticiscat, illis dumtaxat sub Augustaliano iudicio pulsandis, qui ex Caesarii et Attici consulatu possessiones sub patrocinio possidere coeperunt. Quos tamen omnes functionibus publicis obsecundare censemus, ut patronorum nomen extinctum penitus iudicetur. Possessiones autem athuc in suo statu constitutae penes priores possessores residebunt, si pro antiquitate census functiones publicas et liturgos, quos homologi coloni praestare noscuntur, pro rata sunt absque dubio cognituri.

[2] de Zulueta, on whose discussion mine is based, regards the first sentence as referring to titles acquired by patronage *recently*, the last sentences as quieting titles thus acquired before 397. It is perhaps more natural to take the first sentence as referring not to patrons, but to coloni who had submitted to patronage. Otherwise the following clause *quos tamen*, etc., would mean that men who were to lose the land should still pay taxes on it. The reference to abolishing the name of patron comes in quite naturally if the clause means that the coloni involved were to be punished and not to submit to patronage in the future.

[3] See *infra*, p. 134.

viding that they were to remain under public jurisdiction and that no outsiders were to own them or any land in them. A clause further on granted the churches of Constantinople and Alexandria the privilege of retaining lands acquired up to a later date, sometime between 405 and 415, with the proviso that they would be held to whatever public duties *metrocomiae* and public villages owed.[1] These provisions incidentally inform us that whole villages had passed or were in danger of passing under patronage.

On account of the small number of papyri of the fifth century which have been found, we have no picture of how estates were built up after 415. The process does not seem to have been checked by the law. When the curtain rises on the social history of Byzantine Egypt at the end of the century we find the large estates of the period in existence. Fortunately we have considerable information from what must have been, in its own day, one of the most important of these estates, that of the Apion family.

[1] C. T. xi, 24, 6 (1, 6).

## CHAPTER II

### The Apion Family

Officials, as has been noted, were among the most frequent patrons and founders of estates. It is not improbable that the first Apion is to be identified with " Apio Theodosius Johannes, illustrious count of the sacred consistory and *praeses* of the province of Arcadia," who held office about 488.[1] The family clearly appears in 497, when a document from Oxyrhynchus mentions " Flavius Strategius . . . son of the most magnificent and all-esteemed consular Apion." [2] We also know of a collector of the estate of Apion at Heracleopolis in the same year.[3]

So the first head of the family comes into view already a large landowner. He was undoubtedly an Egyptian, as will appear shortly, but his official and personal career for at least half his life is hidden from us. Apion now rose into the sphere of imperial politics, in which the family was to play some part for three generations. The identification, on which this statement depends, of the first three heads of the

[1] P. Ox. 1877; 1888. The Flavius Strategius who was *praeses* of the Thebaid in 349 cannot be connected with this family. Most of his interesting career was outside Egypt, and he is only one of at least six Strategii known in the fourth century. See Otto Seeck, *Die Briefe des Libanius* in O. v. Gebhardt and Adolf Harnack, *Texte und Untersuchungen zur Geschichte der altchristlichen Literatur*, vol. 30, Leipzig, 1906, pp. 282-284.

[2] P. Ox. 1982.

[3] P. Stud. Pal. xx, 129; *cf.* the similar personage in P. Klein. Form. 772 (*Studien zur Palaeographie und Papyruskunde*, vols. iii and viii, Leipzig, 1904 and 1908).

family with three men of the same name who figure in the history of the period is practically certain. The Apion II of the papyri [1] was undoubtedly the consul of 539, and numerous coincidences provide cumulative evidence for his father and grandfather.

Apion I was quartermaster-general of the Persian expedition which the emperor Anastasius sent out in 503. The historian Procopius tells us, after enumerating the generals in command of the various divisions of the expedition, that

> Apion, an Egyptian, a most energetic man and distinguished among the patricians, was sent out to be in charge of the supplies, and the emperor in writing declared him to be a sharer of the imperial power, so that he should have authority to administer these affairs as he wished.[2]

The failure of the expedition ended his career for the time being. He was dismissed, taken to Nicaea, and there by force ordained presbyter. Fourteen years later, on the accession of Justin I in 518, he was recalled to Constantinople and became Praetorian Prefect, a position still practically equivalent to that of prime minister.[3]

It would be interesting if we knew how Apion's career was related to the politics of the time. We have no detailed information, though we may be fairly certain of at least one

1 The heads of the Apion family are here designated by the numbers given them in the note to P. Ox. 1829, 24, where they were first listed in full. They seem to have alternated the names Strategius and Apion for six generations.

2 Procopius, *De Bello Persico* in Procopius, *Opera Omnia*, ed. J. Haury, Leipzig, 1905-1913, 3 vols., i, 8 (105). The fact is also mentioned in Theophanes, *Chronographia*, A. M. 5997 (J.-P. Migne, *Patrologia Graeca*, vol. 108, Paris, 1863, cols. 55-1010; col 349).

3 Theophanes, *Chronographia*, A. M. 5998, 6011 (Migne, P. G. vol. 108, cols. 349, 384-385), *Chronicon Paschale*, 519 (Migne, P. G., vol. 92, cols. 70-1028; col. 859), John Malalas, *Chronographia* (Migne, P. G., vol. 97, cols. 65-718; cols. 587, 607). Malalas, doubtless merely by mistake, speaks of Apion as already Praetorian Prefect in 503.

way in which Apion accommodated himself to the prevailing party. The change from a pro-eastern to a western policy which came with the accession of Justin I meant, under the conditions of 518, a change from monophysitism to orthodoxy.[1] This is, therefore, the most probable place for Apion's "conversion," which his son describes some years later in a speech to a group of monophysite bishops:

You yourselves know that my father Appius [*sic*] of glorious memory, himself a native of the province of Egypt and a follower of your sect and of that of the Alexandrians [the bishops addressed were Syrians] hesitated to communicate with the holy great church established in this city [Constantinople], but the most pious and faithful emperors persuaded him, by this argument, that the most reverend bishops who met at Chalcedon handed down to us no other creed or other faith than that which was confirmed at Nicaea, at Constantinople, and at Ephesus,—they also established the faith and condemned Nestorius and Eutyches, who were introducing new heresies; persuaded by this argument he communicated with the holy church.[2]

It is worth noting that the point on which Apion needed assurance was the acceptance of the fourth general council. Rejection of Chalcedon had come to be one of the most obvious marks of a loyal monophysite and a patriotic Egyptian.[3]

Apion was probably already quite old when he reached the dignity of prefect. He still held it on December 1, 518,[4] but may well have been dead by November 9 of the follow-

[1] Maspero, *Histoire*, pp. 65-69.

[2] Letter of Innocent, bishop of Maronia, in J. D. Mansi, ed., *Sacrorum Conciliorum Nova et Amplissima Collectio*, vol. viii, Florence, 1762, cols. 817-834, col. 818. Innocent himself heard this speech at the conference of 533, referred to *infra*, p. 29.

[3] *Cf.* Maspero, *Histoire*, pp. 20-21; Butler, *Arab Conquest*, p. 185.

[4] C. J. vii, 63(3) (*Corpus Juris Civilis*, Berlin, vol. ii, *Codex Iustinianus*, ed. P. Krueger, 9th ed., 1915).

ing year when Marinus appears in the office.[1] As far as we know, Apion I was largely responsible for the rise of his family to the position it was to occupy for the next century. Very few documents from the estate come from his time, but he almost certainly had established it firmly before the excitements of the last two decades of his life began.

Apion's son, Strategius I, first appears in 497 as Count of the Devoted Domestics and a landowner at Oxyrhynchus.[2] For twenty years he disappears from view, and we can only assume that he shared his father's prosperity and fall. He again comes into sight as prefect of Egypt shortly before 523. This information comes from a reference in Justinian's reforming edict of 538 in which the augustal duke of Egypt is directed to revive the system in the budget of Alexandria which was in force under the administration of Strategius and until fifteen years before the edict was issued.[3] The obvious conclusion is that Strategius held the office of Augustal prefect some time before the year 523.[4] He certainly would not have been appointed before the accession of Justin, nor can he have held the position very long, since there was at least one other prefect between 518 and 523.[5]

We know no definite facts about Strategius' administra-

[1] C. J. v, 27 (7).

[2] Were the palatine titles which Egyptian notables often held real or honorary? *Cf.* Rouillard, *op. cit.*, p. 38.

[3] Edict xiii, 15-16.

[4] The objection that the edict gives Strategius the title *gloriosissimus*, which belonged only to officials higher than the prefect was raised by Luigi Cantarelli "La serie dei prefetti de Egitto: iii Dalla morte di Teodosio I alla conquista araba," in *Atti della R. Accademia dei Lincei*, serie quinta, memorie della classa di scienze morali, storiche, e filologiche, vol. xiv, 385-440; p. 413. The objection is to be answered by pointing out that the edict would use the title which Strategius held when it was issued.

[5] The prefect Licinius, Cantarelli, *op. cit.*, pp. 412-413.

tion. The office of prefect of Egypt was still one of the most important and dignified in the empire, although its powers had been reduced to the civil governorship of the western delta, with a primacy rather than any real power over the other Egyptian provinces.[1] The political situation in Egypt at the moment was that the government had not yet dared to interfere with the national monophysite party, which it was vigorously suppressing in Syria, and the Coptic church and patriarch were therefore able to offer a safe retreat to refugees from other parts of the empire.[2] Conditions must have called for skillful handling by the prefect.

Our knowledge of the life of Strategius may be compared to what we might see of a train whose route lay mainly through tunnels, with only short open spaces between. We do not know what he was doing for twenty years before he became prefect, and there is another gap of at least ten years after his administration. From the rank which Strategius attained in the last years of his life we may infer that he held positions of some importance in the imperial service. He comes into view again in 533, when Justinian chose him to preside as his representative over a conference of six orthodox and six oriental (monophysite) bishops which was held at Constantinople in the vain hope of effecting a reconciliation. "The conference is not to be in my presence, to save my dignity," said Justinian at the opening, "but I shall instruct the most glorious patrician Strategius to sit with you."[3]

[1] Gelzer, *op. cit.*, pp. 20-21.

[2] Maspero, *op. cit.*, pp. 69-74, 100-101.

[3] Letter of Innocent, Bishop of Maronia, in Mansi, *op. cit.*, vol. viii, col. 817. The date of the conference, which could formerly only be given as between 533 and 536, is now definitely fixed at 533 by the fact that Strategius became Count of the Sacred Largesses before the end of that year, as stated *infra*, p. 30. *Cf.* Maspero, *Histoire*, p. 99, note 3.

The bishop to whom we owe our account of this conference refers to Strategius as the "*gloriosissimus patricius Strategius qui nunc comes divinarum ubique largitionum est*"; elsewhere he adds "*eo tempore loco tuebatur gloriosi magistri officii.*"[1] The obvious meaning of these expressions is that he acted for a time as Master of the Offices,[2] perhaps as *locum tenens* of that high position during a vacancy, and afterward became Count of the Sacred Largesses. As head of the imperial treasury and one of the high officers of state, Strategius had now reached the climax of his career.

Strategius was Count of the Largesses from 533 to 538. The first of these dates is fixed by the only Greek protocol which has yet been entirely diciphered. The protocol was the official record on the first volumn of a roll of papyrus, and contained the name of the Count of the Sacred Largesses, in whose department the government papyrus factories fell. A law of 537 required a protocol on all legal documents, but the practice was evidently not a new one.[3] In the protocol in question here the title is "Flavius Strategius, most glorious consular and general," the date Phaophi 9, twelfth indiction.[4] The Byzantine habit of using the indiction as sufficient date is responsible for the fact that this document tells us only that it was written in the twelfth year of the current fifteen-year census period. The only indiction year, however, which falls near the dates otherwise known for Strategius' term of office is that which began in September, 533. This protocol, therefore, the first dated document which mentions Strategius in his high office, was written on

[1] *Ibid.*, 818, 817.

[2] For which office see A. E. R. Boak, "The Master of the Offices," in A. E. R. Boak and James Dunlap, *Two Studies in Later Roman and Byzantine Administration*, New York, 1924, pp. vii-160.

[3] Nov. 44.

[4] P. Ox. 1928.

October 6, 533. Strategius is mentioned in several of the laws issued in the next few years,[1] his last appearance being in Edict XIII. In that document he is evidently spoken of as still alive. Since it dates from the indiction year which began September 1, 538,[2] and Strategius' son was consul for 539, almost certainly after his father's death,[3] the date of that event, and incidentally the date of the edict, may be fixed with almost complete certainty in the last four months of the year 538.

The years 533-538 were among the most important of Justinian's reign. Strategius was in office when the Code in its final form was promulgated and the great victories of Belisarius were being won, when Justinian was undertaking the reorganization of the provinces, and when St. Sophia was being built.[4] A peace with Persia had been concluded just before his term and ended just after it. Procopius mentions Strategius, " a patrician and archon of the imperial treasury, and besides a man of wisdom and noble birth," as one of the two officials whom Justinian sent to settle a dispute between pro-Roman and pro-Persian Arabs which was one of the causes of the outbreak of war. The historian credits him with the advice, most appropriate for a man in his position, not to waste the empire's money on fighting for a small and unproductive piece of land.[5]

Other indications besides the high offices which he held and the responsible commissions with which he was intrusted show the position Strategius had reached. Edict XIII

[1] Nov. 136 (April 1, 535) ; 22 (March 18, 536) ; 105 (December 28, 537).

[2] See *supra*, p. 18, note 1.

[3] See *infra*, p. 32.

[4] For these events see J. B. Bury, *History of the Later Roman Empire*, London, 1923, 2 vols., vol. ii, pp. 48-54, 124-139, 170-195, 334-346, 396-398.

[5] Procopius, *De Bello Persico*, ii, 1 (9-11). The phase quoted above is as near as Procopius' principles will allow him to get Strategius' Latin title.

takes his Egyptian administration as a norm on certain matters in a way which probably either is a personal compliment or means that he was the government's adviser and source of information on the subject in question.[1] A similar indication is the very fact that Strategius' son, Apion II, held the consulship in 539. Apion, as far as we know, occupied no important imperial office either before or after, and yet he stands in the list of consuls between the Praetorian Prefect and the emperor's cousin, Justin.[2] The significant way in which the *Chronicon Paschale* notes him as " Apion, son of Strategius," while all the other consuls appear with their own names alone, certainly supports the idea that he was given the dignity in his father's memory, quite possibly to fill a position originally planned for Strategius himself.[3]

Apparently Strategius managed to be pagarch of Oxyrhynchus and Heracleopolis while he was Count of the Sacred Largesses, presumably exercising his local functions by deputy.[4] We may be sure in any case that he did not neglect

[1] Edict xiii, 15-16. Some such explanation is necessary, since Strategius is not mentioned as the originator of the system which is to be revived,—" everything is to be paid which was given up to the time of the most glorious Strategius, nor shall the honorable Augustal make any greater expense than was customary before and during the time of the most glorious Strategius . . . but he shall preserve the old system which existed before and under the most glorious Strategius,"—nor as the last under whom it was enforced,—" this system remained not only through the administration of the most glorious Strategius, but up to the second indiction of the last cycle, fifteen years ago."

[2] List of consuls in Willy Liebenam, *Fasti Consulares Imperii Romani* in *Kleine Texte für Theologische und Philologische Vorlesungen und Übungen*, 41-43, Bonn, 1909. On Justin, consul in 540, see Delbrueck, *Consulardiptychen*, vol. i, pp. 151-152; Bury, *History*, vol. ii, p. 70.

[3] After a lapse of two years the consulship had been revived in 538 and first held by the Praetorian Prefect John; on the last years of the consulship see Bury, *op. cit.*, vol. ii, pp. 346-348.

[4] P. Ox. 1983 (535) is addressed to Strategius as πρωτεύων at Oxyrhynchus and Heracleopolis. The title appears as the equivalent of pagarch in P. Stud. Pal. xx, 128.

his interests at home. A wine account from the Apion estate in which we hear of wine sent to Constantinople " to our master " perhaps comes from his time, in which case we know from another item in the document that his birthday was January 23.[1]

Under whatever circumstances, Flavius Apion II reached what was still the highest dignity in the empire.[2] Only two other subjects held the consular title after him, and it must have given the clerks on his estate a great feeling of pride to be able to write for the rest of his life, " Flavius Apion, the all-esteemed and most magnificent ex-consul—ordinarius and patrician, and a land owner at this illustrious city of Oxyrhynchus," [3] or to endorse items of expenditure " by written order of our master the consul." [4]

Except for this one flourish the career of Apion II seems to have been entirely confined to Egypt. Quite possibly it was in his father's lifetime that he was defensor of Oxyrhynchus.[5] In 549-550 he was duke of the Thebaid,[6] and probably at various times held the positions of pagarch and tribune in the districts where his estates lay. We know definitely that he held both offices at Arsinoe in 556,[7] and it

[1] PSI, 953, 72-73, 80-81 (G. Vitelli, *Papiri greci e latini, Pubblicazioni della societá italiana per la ricerca dei papiri greci e latini in Egitto*, Florence, 9 vols., 1912-1929).

[2] His consular diptych is CIL ii 2699, reproduced as the frontispiece. Documents dated by his consulship are Nov. 78; CIG iv 8635; P. Cairo 67106; 67255; PSI 188; P. Berlin Möller 3 (Sigurd Möller, *Griechische Papyri aus dem Berliner Museum*, Göteborg, 1929).

[3] P. Ox. 134.

[4] P. Ox. 1911, 148.

[5] P. Ox. 1886.

[6] P. Ox. 130; the date is given by P. Lond. 1708 (see note on line 79) of 567, which refers to the second year of Apion as seventeen years before.

[7] BGU 305 (*Ägyptische Urkunden aus den Königlichen Museen zu Berlin*, Berlin, 1895-1926, 7 vols.).

seems probable that he was pagarch at Oxyrhynchus at the time of his death.[1] It is in his time that we begin to have documents from the estate in fairly large numbers. While undoubtedly he inherited interests already built up by his father and grandfather, we may probably think of him as actively interested in the management of his property. At least we know that he occasionally visited it.[2]

Apion II died between 577 and 579. The dates are fixed by the last document addressed to him and the first addressed to his heirs.[3] Apion II evidently directed, or else his heirs agreed on, some scheme of joint ownership. Such arrangements seem to have been rather common in Egypt at the time; for in an Oxyrhynchus tax list thirteen out of twenty-eight proprietors are groups of heirs;[4] and even coloni appear, according to some of the Apion accounts, to have made similar settlements.[5] So "the most magnificent heirs of the late Apion, protopatrician, of glorious memory, landowners at this illustrious city of Oxyrhynchus"[6] are the owners of the estate for the next few years. The chief of them was probably Apion's son, Strategius II. He had been important on the estate long before his father's death. An appeal written by a colonus as early as 550 associates him with his father,—"I will send up unceasing hymns to the Lord Christ for the life of your lordship and that of your most magnificent son, the Lord Strategius,"[7] and in 557 he is mentioned as authorizing expenditure.[8] To him is prob-

[1] P. Ox. 1829.

[2] P. Ox. 1913, 59-60.

[3] P. Ox. 1896 and 135 respectively.

[4] P. Ox. 2020.

[5] *E. g.*, P. Ox. 1912, 34-36, 38, 50, etc.; PSI 954.

[6] P. Ox. 1976.

[7] P. Ox. 130.

[8] P. Ox. 1911, 150-151.

ably addressed a letter referring to the opening of his father's will.[1] Unfortunately no further records of his life remain.

Flavius Apion III and his mother, Praejecta, are the owners of the estate in 591. Apion III then appears alone between 593 and 619.[2] A third Strategius, who is mentioned between 615 and 625, is the last known member of the family.[3]

This Strategius III is probably to be identified with a nobleman who figures in the church history of the period.[4] In 616 Athanasius, the monophysite patriarch of Antioch, was in Alexandria attempting to arrange a union between the Syrian and Egyptian churches. It was by no means surprising that those bodies which had broken off from the emperor's church along national lines should go a step further and separate from each other.[5] Nicetas, who had conquered Egypt six years before for the new emperor, Heraclius, was favorable to the project of reunion. Nevertheless, after several fruitless conversations Athanasius had almost given up hope. At this point the patrician Strategius arrived in Alexandria from Arsinoe [6] and took a strong inter-

[1] P. Ox. 1829.

[2] Praejecta and Apion in P. Ox. 1989-1990; Apion P. Ox. 201 (593 A. D.); P. Iand. 49 (619 A. D., C. Kalbfleisch and others, *Papyri Iandanae*, Leipzig, 1912-14, 4 fasc.)

[3] BGU 368 (615 A. D.); P. Stud. Pal, xx, 209 (625 A. D.) See discussion of the date in P. Ox. 1829, note to line 24.

[4] J. B. Chabot, *Chronique de Michel le Syrien*, Paris, 1901-1924, 4 vols., vol. ii, pp. 385-393, iv. 395-398. Jean Maspero, *Histoire*, p. 330 proposes the identification, which is accepted by H. I. Bell ("The Decay of a Civilization" in the *Journal of Egyptian Archaeology*, vol. x, pp. 207-216, p. 212). The name occurs in Syriac and could be read "Strategius the patrician" or "the general Patricius." The title follows the name in the case of Nicetas in the same passage.

[5] For the incident in general see Maspero, *Histoire*, chaps. ix-x.

[6] Strategius is described as a patrician of Arsinoe in BGU 368 and P. Stud. Pal. xx, 209.

est in the matter. Meetings were held in his presence between representatives of the two sides. Strategius insisted on their reaching an agreement and had his secretary take down the articles of union as they were formulated. It was largely owing to his zeal that the last difficulties were overcome and the union actually brought about.

So the Apion family describes, as it were, a complete circle in its history. Originating in Egypt, it rose for a while into the larger world of the empire, and was then again restricted to its native country. The political history of the family is paralleled by the history of their relations to the church. As Apion I passed from the Coptic to the imperial and Greek orthodox church, so some later member of the family must have returned to the national Egyptian body of which Strategius III was such a leading member.

With all our information on the Apion estate, we have but little light on the personalities of its owners. We may perhaps detect family traditions in two matters. The first has to do with relations to the church, which have just been mentioned. Apion I changed his allegiance when circumstances demanded it. Strategius I hopefully quoted that example to a group of monophysite bishops. Strategius II swept away with obvious impatience the differences of the Syrian and Egyptian churches:

> Why do we wrongly and unjustly harm each other? Why do we not put an end to the causeless dispute, heal this schism, and make peace with our brothers, the orientals?[1]

All had at least this in common, that they attached greater importance to other considerations than to the theological and national disputes of the time. The other family tradition was one of preparing the heir for his future headship of the estate. The three Strategii all appear, even while

[1] Chabot, *op. cit.*, vol. ii, p. 387.

their fathers were alive, as landowners or persons of authority on the estate.

The re-Egyptianization of the Apion family was evidently quite complete in the seventh century. This is sufficiently evident from the fact that they retained their property after the Persians had conquered the country from the Roman empire. Documents from the period of the Persian occupation show the Apion estate in regular operation.[1]

With the references of the Persian period the family disappears from view, nor do we know how it came to an end. Very probably the Apions found it too hard to keep their footing in the rapid changes of the seventh century, and were either punished as Copts and supporters of Persia when Egypt was regained, or lost their estates at the Arabic conquest.

[1] P. Ox. 1921 (621 A. D.); P. Stud. Pal. xx, 209 (625 A. D.); *cf.* Edward Rochie Hardy, Jr., "New Light on the Persian Conquest of Egypt," in the *Journal of the Society of Oriental Research*, vol. xiii, pp. 185-189.

## THE APION FAMILY

(Based on the Family Tree given in the Notes to P. Ox. 1829)

Apion I

(First mentioned 497, last as Praetorian Prefect 518)

Strategius I

(First appears *com. dev. dom.* 497, died *com. sacr. larg.*, 538)

Apion II = Cyra (?) (Survived)

(Consul ordinarius, 539, died between 577 and 579)

Strategius II = Flavia Praejecta(?) — Son (Name not given) — Theognosia

(Alive 548–9 probably dead by 590)

Apion III

(Appears 590–619)

Strategius III

(Mentioned by papyri and Syriac historian 615–625)

Note.—The mutual relation of the last three heads of the family is still, of course, somewhat conjectural.

# CHAPTER III

## Other Proprietors of the Period

The Apion family was undoubtedly but one among many large landowners in Byzantine Egypt, although it was certainly among the most important. We have glimpses of a number of other estates and considerable information about a few of them. It must also be remembered that Egypt still contained landed properties of every size, from the large estate to the peasants' holding, as in earlier periods in its history.

The Apion documents do not illustrate the actual rise of a family into the landowning class. Another series of Oxyrhychus papyri exemplifies this stage in the history of another family. We first meet the palatine Flavius Eulogius as an owner of house property at Oxyrhynchus in 476.[1] The palatine was a local representative of the Count of the Sacred Largesses, and Eulogius had presumably been stationed in this part of the country.[2] It appears from a legal document that he also loaned money on the security of houses at Oxyrhynchus.[3] His sons, Apphous and Martyrius, continued his business interests, as we learn from a lease of 487.[4] In 495 Flavius Apphous, who eight years before had been

[1] P. Ox. 1958.

[2] We may perhaps infer from this document that there were other *palatini* in Egypt besides the one at Alexandria who received the taxes (Rouillard, *op. cit.*, p. 110). But their functions are doubtful. On the office in general see C. J. xii, 23

[3] P. Ox. 1876.

[4] P. Ox. 1961.

content with the plebeian *nomen* Aurelius, appears as tribune.[1] Four years later he owns houses in the village of Senocomis and is addressed as a landowner, γεουχῶν.[2] The title is that regularly used for estate owners,—the heads of the Apion family, for example. The same title is applied to the two brothers in 500, to Apphous again in 511, and to "Flavius Hatres, most illustrious son of the late Martyrius" in 518.[3] Flavius Serenus, son of Martyrius, was tribune in 525. In a contract of 550 for the management of his stable he is addressed as "most magnificent and distinguished count of the consistory and landowner at this illustrious city of Oxyrhynchus."[4]

A few other cases may be cited of landowners at Oxyrhynchus who come into view for a moment. Flavius Alexander, the most magnificent and most glorious general, appears as the owner of the κτῆμα of Piaa in 476. He must have had considerable holdings in at least two nomes, since the Flavius Joseph who acts for him in this document is only described as dioecetes of his Oxyrhynchus property.[5] About a century later we meet Flavia Euphemia, whose estate was large enough to require a special rent-collector as well as a general dioecetes.[6] The Arcadian estate of her contemporary Flavia Christodota, daughter of the patrician John, was endangered by a debtor's non-payment of an obligation for the respectable sum of sixty-one pounds of gold.[7] Two

[1] P. Ox. 1891.

[2] P. Ox. 1959. P. Lond. 1876 is probably another lease addressed to Flavius Apphous as landowner and son of the late palatine Eulogius.

[3] P. Ox. 1962; 1960; PSI 466.

[4] P. Iand. 43; P. Ox. 140.

[5] P. Ox. 1899.

[6] P. Ox. 1038 (568 A. D.).

[7] PSI 76 (574-578 A. D.).

lists, also dating from about 570, enumerate in connection with payments to the government over twenty such persons as the most glorious Ptolemy, the most magnificent Athanasia, the most glorious Cometus, the most glorious Patricia, and the most glorious Justus and his brothers.[1] A high proportion of women is noticeable, as well as a number of cases where groups of heirs were in possession. Our only indication of the size of any of these properties is an account of the most magnificent Christodora of Cynopolis, whose expenses in grain reached the sum of 40,117⅛ artabae in one year.[2] We may note for comparison that the highest figure for grain receipts in any of the several cases where we have a year's accounts from one of the numerous districts into which the Apion estate is divided is 5054 artabae.[3] Only in two cases outside of the Apion and Eulogius families do we happen to know of an estate existing for more than one generation.[4] Doubtless this is due to the scattered nature of our information, and we may take it for granted that these landowners did their best to hand their property on to their descendants. A special problem which comes up in connection with the landowners of the Oxyrhynchite nome is discussed at the end of the chapter.

The Fayum has unfortunately not given us a large series of documents from any one estate. There are enough traces of landowners, however, to show that there also the Apion family was by no means alone. The patrician Sophia, who managed business matters also for her glorious son, presum-

[1] P. Ox. 2020; 2040. The date is fixed by the appearance of Euphemia in 2040 and of Cometus, whom Christodota mentions in PSI 76 as her brother, in both documents. The titles are probably purely honorary.

[2] P. Ox. 2026.

[3] P. Ox. 1910, 1.

[4] Theon appears in P. Ox. 1999 and other documents. His daughter is a house-owner at Oxyrhynchus in P. Ox. 1965 and PSI 709. Musaeus is mentioned in P. Ox. 2039, his daughter Euphemia in P. Ox. 1038.

ably a boy under age, is known from a group of orders for payment addressed to a notary, the objects of expenditure closely paralleling those found in the Apion accounts.[1] Flavius Marous is unfortunately known only from a few fragmentary documents.[2] Flavius Eustochius, most magnificent son of Count Cyril and landowner at Arsinoë in 532, is perhaps to be connected with the Flavius Eustochius who was civil governor of the district in 487.[3] In the early seventh century Flavius Theodosacius was pagarch and tribune and the owner of house property at Arsinoë.[4] Doubtless there were estates of such personages all over the Arsinoite nome. An interesting account comes from a property controlled by a woman whose name has not been preserved.[5] Finally, there is a quite tantalizing letter written by two collectors who describe themselves, probably rhetorically, as slaves of their mistress, the most magnificent Patricia (or *patricia*). After generalities they start to tell her about the violence they suffered on the feast of their patron, St. . . . at which point the document breaks off.[6]

A glance at the map will show how the other estates of which we know were scattered over the whole of Egypt. From an estate at Hermopolis, in the northern Thebaid, comes a long account covering the business of four years.[7] Unfortunately we can only describe this property, when it is

[1] P. Klein Form. 1091-1097.

[2] P. Klein Form. 246-252.

[3] P. Stud. Pal. xx 140; 128.

[4] BGU 3; 320.

[5] P. Stud. Pal. x 251. (*Studien zur Palaeographie und Papyruskunde*, vol. x, Leipzig, 1910).

[6] BGU 798.

[7] P. Bad. 95 (Friedrich Bilabel, *Griechische Papyri* in *Veröffentlichungen aus den badischen Papyrus-Sammlungen*, hft. 4, Heidelberg, 1924), brilliantly studied by M. Schnebel in " An Agricultural Ledger in P. Bad. 95 " in *The Journal of Egyptian Archaeology*, vol. xiv, pp. 34-45.

referred to in the rest of this study, as the Hermopolis estate, since it is not clear who the owners were. Three counts received the net income at the end, and a mistress appears in the body of the document, but their exact relation to the estate and to each other is not evident.

Further south the sixth-century papyri from Aphrodito give us some information from the estate of a certain most magnificent Count Ammonius,[1] perhaps a *praeses* of the Thebaid.[2] Other documents in the series show us a group of decurions of Antaeopolis who owned property in other parts of the nome.[3] The privileges of the village of Aphrodito itself are one of our chief sources on the legal and administrative status of Egyptian landowners of our period; and at least some of the villagers rose sufficiently in the world to belong to the lesser gentry.[4] Three Byzantine ostraca carry orders for the issue of oil written by a dioecetes, probably of a private estate.[5] Finally, almost at the very border of Roman Egypt, a charitable institution at Ombos was built by the duke, various officials, and the πρῶτοι of the place.[6]

Having rapidly surveyed the private estates in different parts of Byzantine Egypt, we may now look at the public proprietors. Of these there are two, the state, or rather the emperor, and the church. The royal or public land, which under the first Ptolemies was practically the whole of Egypt, had been shrinking ever since. By the Byzantine period the

[1] P. Cairo 67062; 67138-67139, etc.

[2] P. Cairo 67323.

[3] P. Cairo 67327, etc.

[4] The phrase is applied to the poet Dioscorus in Bell and Crum, "A Greek-Coptic Glossary."

[5] Ulrich Wilcken, *Griechische Ostraka aus Aegypten und Nubien*, Leipzig, 1899, nos. 1603-1605.

[6] Rec. Chret. 561 (Gustave Lefebvre, *Recueil des inscriptions grecques-chrétiennes d'Égypte*, Cairo, 1907).

"divine house" was only one of the proprietors of Egypt and probably not the most important. The imperial estate seems to occur in our documents on the same level with others. A letter speaks of "the divine house and the house of the all-esteemed Patricia" as if they were similar establishments.[1] In Apion documents we hear of occasional contacts between the Apion and imperial property. Tenants of the divine house rent Apion land; Apion serfs escape to an imperial manor; the two estate administrations collaborate in a criminal investigation.[2]

Imperial estate officials are in our period sometimes called δεσποτικοὶ or δεσποινικοί. We hear of them in Oxyrhynchus and at Aphrodito, where the whole village, by placing itself under the patronage of the empress, seems to have become, at least technically, part of the imperial domain.[3] Of the inner workings of the domain administration we have only a few glimpses. In the Oxyrhychite nome a general manager of the imperial property still existed in the fifth and sixth centuries, and documents of 420-421 mention a wine-seller and a rent-collector among his subordinates.[4] In the sixth century one of the imperial properties, like those of the Apion family, was managed by a pronoetes.[5]

The property of the church was probably more extensive. It was largely formed by pious donations, both public and private. The emperors were occasionally generous, and the Egyptians of this period often remembered the church in their wills.[6] In most aspects of administration

[1] PSI 238.

[2] P. Ox. 1915; 2056; 1853.

[3] P. Ox. 1853; P. Cairo 67088; 67283.

[4] P. Ox. 1134; 1892; 1973.

[5] PSI 196-197.

[6] Every will of the period yet found had some legacy to the church; *e. g.*, P. Ox. 1901; P. Cairo 67151; 67312.

ecclesiastical estates did not differ greatly from secular, and will be used for illustration along with the latter in later chapters. A few special features of the administration of church property may be noted here. It was frequently rented on hereditary (emphyteutic) leases.[1] The word δίκαιον is used in a rather confusing way, sometimes for the business administration of an ecclesiastical body,[2] sometimes for a church or monastery in its corporate personality.[3] The title oeconomus was used exclusively for the business manager of a church or monastery. We have references to oeconomi of the church of Alexandria,[4] of the churches of Oxyrhynchus[5] and Tentyra,[6] and of various parish churches in town and country.[7] It is obvious that the importance of an oeconomus would vary greatly as between, let us say, an oeconomus of the church of Alexandria and the oeconomus of Apa Psoius' in the village of Ibion.[8] The more important dioceses had a fairly well-organized estate administration. We have a few references to the way in which the church of Hermopolis divided up its business,[9] and some information from the church of Oxyrhynchus, which

[1] P. Lond. 483; P Cairo 67298-67299; *cf.* P. Klein. Form 47; 272; 314.

[2] *Cf.* P. Cairo 67298.

[3] *E. g.*, P. Cairo 67096; P. Lond. 1686.

[4] Leontius of Neapolis, *Life of St. John the Almoner*, ed. Heinrich Gelzer, *Leontios' von Neapolis Leben des heiligen Johannes des Barmherzigen, Erzbischofs von Alexandrien* in *Sammlung ausgewählter kirchen- und dogmengeschichtlicher Quellen*, hft. 5, Freiburg, 1893; 1, etc.

[3] *E. g.*, P. Cairo 67096; P. Lond. 1686.

[6] P. Cairo 67298.

[7] *E. g.*, P. Lond. 1028; P. Ox. 1917, fol. 2.

[8] P. Grenfell ii, 111. (Bernard P. Grenfell and Arthur S. Hunt, *New Classical Fragments and Other Greek and Latin Papyri*, Greek Papyri, series ii, Oxford, 1897).

[9] Note the hierarchy in P. Klein Form. 271, and the evidence for districts of the estate in P. Lond. 1782-1785.

had a general oeconomus and under him various officials in charge of villages, etc.[1] A series of orders for the issue of oil comes from the Fayum, probably from the property of the church of Arsinoe.[2] They give us a picture of the running of a large establishment, its salaries and special expenses. Some of our evidence suggests that the dioceses had some financial rights and control over the property of the churches within them.[3]

Monasteries were among the most important ecclesiastical proprietors. The abbot managed the business of his monastery. In establishments of any size one of the monks acted as oeconomus, under the direction of the superior, and with such assistance as might be called for by the amount of property involved.[4] A will from Antinoë, wishing to refer as fully as possible to those in control of the property of a monastery, speaks of the superior, oeconomi, and dioecetae for the time being.[5] Monks would be sent as special or permanent representatives to look after the monastery's interests at a distance. Thus two *apocrisarii* of a monastery at Hermopolis, for instance, delivered the wine which it sold to a Libyan bishop.[6] Probably among the wealthiest ecclesiastical bodies was the monastery of the Metanoia at Canopus, a suburb of Alexandria. It received annually an income of grain from the taxes, probably assigned to it by imperial

[1] P. Ox. 1900; 1894.

[2] P. Klein Form. 898-945, 1074-1076. The ecclesiastical connection appears from 932 "the oil of the church" and 940 "account of the holy church of Rodeon for repairs." On the other hand, orders are clearly given by a single "God-protected lord," not by a corporation; hence the estate was probably that controlled by the bishop.

[3] P. Bad. 94; P. Klein Form. 302; P. Grenfell ii, 111.

[4] *Cf.* P. Lond. 483; 1690; P. Cairo 67096; 67170-67171; 67299; P. Flor. 285.

[5] P. Cairo 67151, 146-7.

[6] P. Cairo 67168, 64-65.

grant; 5759 artabae, for instance, came from the village of Aphrodito. It collected this revenue in its own boats under the supervision of its διακονηταί. We know of two of these officials, themselves monks of the Metanoia, who were assigned to the Antaeopolite nome; and presumably there were others in other parts of Egypt.[1] Hospitals, xenodocheia, and presumably other charitable institutions had their own oeconomi.[2]

As might be expected clerics appear frequently in the management of church property and nearly always hold the controlling positions. There are, however, plenty of cases of laymen in the service of the church.[3]

## Excursus

### The οἶκοι at Oxyrhynchus

It is doubtful whether a certain group of Oxyrhynchus documents refer to private estates or to administrative divisions. The series in question speaks of various "houses" in connection with the government of the nome. Thus an application of 572 for revision of the tax registers is addressed "to the tax-collecting office (ἐξακτορικὴ τάξις) of the section (μερίς) and house of Theon of glorious memory."[4] Two parallel documents use the same terms in reference to the house of Timagenes.[5] Two other documents are receipts addressed to the epimeletes of the house of Theon by collectors of embolé for their fees.[6] A list of payments of

[1] References to the Metanoia are collected in the introduction to P. Cairo 67286. P. Lond. 995; 996; 1152; P. Cairo 67347 mention payments of grain to the boat of the Metanoia; P. Cairo 67286 the annual payment from Aphrodito and the διακονηταί.

[2] P. Ox. 1894; PSI 284.

[3] *E. g.*, P. Ox. 1894.

[4] P. Ox. 126.

[5] P. Ox. 1887; P. Warren, there cited.

[6] P. Ox. 1999; 2009.

grain from the houses of Theon, Timagenes, and Eudaemon through the presbyter Daniel perhaps refers to some ecclesiastical due, since the amounts are scarcely large enough to have been the payment in full of any tax.[1] Apart from financial affairs we have a reference to *riparii* of the house of Theon, who were provided for by various other "houses."[2]

It must be remarked that the word οἶκος did not refer to a family, but to a financial administration; thus the divine house was not the dynasty but the imperial estate office.[3] Several interpretations of the documents cited above are possible. It has been suggested that Timagenes and Theon were either "large landowners responsible for the collection of taxes chargeable on their property or . . . official *exactores* whose estates were still accountable, after their death, for the collection in their departments."[4] The only proposal made about the word μερίς on either of these theories is that it refers to their share of family property.[5]

A third interpretation will perhaps cover more of the facts. It is possible that the houses of Theon and the rest were districts into which the Oxyrhynchite nome was divided for certain financial and administrative purposes. The administrative division of nomes was not unknown in the Byzantine period. References to colleagues in the office of pagarch[6] suggest one way in which this was done, although it is not clear in the cases which occur whether the division

[1] P. Ox. 2016.

[2] P. Ox. 2039.

[3] *E. g.*, P. Ox. 1892; PSI 196-197.

[4] P. Ox. 1887, note to line 2.

[5] M. Gelzer, "Altes und Neues aus der byzantinisch-ägyptischen Verwaltungsmisere" in *Archiv für Papyrusforschung*, vol. v, 1913, pp. 346-377; p. 357, note 4.

[6] Antaeopolis, P. Lond. 1661; P. Cairo 67325; perhaps Oxyrhynchus, P. Ox. 2040.

was functional or geographical.[1] At Hermopolis a division of the nome into μερίδες had survived as late as 380.[2] A sixth century receipt acknowledges the payment of a certain Flavius Basil for his services in connection with the embolé for the μερίς of Dioscorides.[3] The nome in this case is unfortunately not designated. It suggests a direct parallel, at any rate, for the districts of Theon and Timagenes. The official character of the latter divisions is strengthened by the title epimeletes, which commonly designates in this period a taxing official of some importance,[4] and has not, I believe, been found in private service. Another case of such subdivisions of nomes may be found in a reference to a *riparius* of the ninth house at Heracleopolis.[5] A rising aristocracy would scarcely submit to be numbered, and we must have here some administrative district, perhaps a survival of the numbered pagi of the fourth century. We may suppose that the names of former officials had come to be attached to the districts at Oxyrhynchus. In any case, this series of documents may be tentatively removed from those relating to landowners as such.

[1] *Cf.* discussion in Rouillard, *op. cit.*, pp. 55-57.

[2] P. Florence 75 (C. Vitelli and D. Comparetti, *Papiri Fiorentini*, Milan, 1906-1915, 3 vols.). For earlier use see Friedrich Preisigke, *Wörterbuch der Griechischen Papyrusurkunden*, Berlin, 1924-1929, vols. 1-3. s. v. The sixth century division of the property of the church of Hermopolis into μερίδες may reflect these districts; P. Lond. 1060; 1072; 1782-5.

[3] P. Leipzig 90 (Ludwig Mitteis, *Griechische Urkunden der Papyrussammlung zu Leipzig*, Leipzig, 1906).

[4] Gelzer, "Altes und Neues," pp. 357-358; *cf.* P. Ox. 1919, 11.

[5] P. Rainer 30, 52 (Carl Wessely, *Corpus Papyrorum Raineri*, vol. i, *Griechische Texte*, Vienna, 1895).

## CHAPTER IV

### FEUDALISM AND SERFDOM

THERE are admittedly many similarities between the economic and social conditions of Byzantine Egypt and those of mediaeval Europe, and the culture and general atmosphere of the period have much that is mediaeval about them.[1] It is necessary, however, to avoid the risk of thinking that the two situations were the same. A number of differences could be pointed out. For instance, Byzantine Egypt still had its Roman municipalities and a bureaucracy, even though the latter was rather creaky. Nor is there much trace of a definite personal tie between lord and serf or between vassal and emperor in the quasi-feudal phenomena which form the subject of this chapter.

Two main groups of phenomena are illustrated. The first is the assumption, or usurpation, of government functions by the landowners; the second, the system of serfdom. Estate intervention in the collection of taxes is perhaps the most important of the former group. Our documents show two ways in which the large landowners had taken over some part of the tax-collecting privilege—by collecting the taxes of their coloni and by acquiring the right of αὐτοπραγία, i.e., self-collection, the right held by certain persons or groups to pay their taxes directly to a central authority and not to the collector in charge of the district. The first of these customs had been recognized as long ago as 366 by a law making the owners of large estates responsible for the taxes of their

[1] *Cf.* H. I. Bell, "The Byzantine Servile State in Egypt," in *The Journal of Egyptian Archaeology*, vol. iv, pp. 86-106.

coloni.[1] In 529 an edict of Justinian refers incidentally to an existing difference of custom. Some coloni paid their taxes directly, while others gave the landlord a lump sum, of which he used part for the taxes and kept part for his own expenses.[2]

This particular system is well illustrated by the accounts from the estate of Count Ammonius in the Thebaid. Sometimes a separate account is kept for each tenant, indicating how much, in grain and money, was collected from him, how much was spent for taxes, and how much remained. Sometimes a detailed list is drawn up of the contributions of the various peasants towards the estate's payment for embolé.[3] Even on this estate, however, the system of setting aside a certain part of the receipts for taxes does not seem to have been always followed. A letter addressed to Count Ammonius' manager, for example, directs him to collect a certain debt and use part of the money either for taxes or for the purchase of reeds.[4]

The same general principle was in force elsewhere. A letter written to an archimandrite, apparently by a tenant of church property, speaks of one of his fellow coloni as paying taxes "to the most holy father." [5] A receipt issued by the oeconomus of a church at Aphrodito mentions rent and taxes together.[6] In an appeal to Apion II one of his coloni speaks of "serving my good master and paying the taxes every year." [7] The Apion accounts seem to indicate that the pay-

[1] C. T. xi, 1 (14).

[2] C J. xi, 48 (20).

[3] P. Cairo 67138, I. R., II. R., III, R.; 67139, II. V.

[4] P. Cairo 67062.

[5] BGU 103.

[6] PSI 937; *cf.* P. Cairo 67307. P. Lond. 1758 mentions the payment of embolé by a peasant through a monastery, perhaps a similar transaction.

[7] P. Ox. 130. The same word is used of the obligations of a colonus in PSI 62.

ments to the government were made out of the total receipts instead of being separated at the source as the money or grain came in from each tenant. It does appear, however, that the peasants sometimes knew what they were paying for. Thus in a fragment of the Apion rent roll an item " for the indictions " appears. It was recorded as a charge on the who community referred to, but was paid by its members severally.[1] " Payment of the head tax (συντέλεια κεφαλῆς) " occurs in a few Apion accounts.[2]

The pronoetae of the Apion estate collected the dues of the peasants but did not themselves make the tax payments. Instead of this they turned their net receipts over " to your magnificence or to your representatives, that is, the grain to the public boatman of your glorious house, the money to the illustrious cashier of the same glorious house." [3] Owing to the policy of the estate, however, which seems to have had little use for surplus grain,[4] the grain which the estate boatmen collected was mainly for embolé. The transaction would be recorded in a receipt like the following:

Receipt of me, Asclas, boatman, of Coma. Pamouthius, pronoetes of Leon, has measured out and placed in the boats under my command 1485 ¼ artabae of good clean wheat by cancellus measure for the embolé of the 13th indiction . . . and for naulage to Alexandria 11 solidi and 3½ karats.[5]

[1] P. Ox. 2037.

[2] PSI 954, 19-21; P. Ox. 1911, 86; 1912, 30.

[3] P. Ox. 136.

[4] See page 100, *infra*.

[5] P. Ox. 142. Apparently the estate paid rather less than its share of naulage; *cf.* Rouillard, *op. cit.*, pp. 145-156. P. Ox. 142; 1913, 61-62 and 2022, 6 suggest it paid naulage for transportation only to Alexandria, not to Constantinople. P. Ox. 1998 is a receipt for embolé paid by John, pronoetes of Coma, to the boatman Menas, perhaps the Menas, son of Asclas, who appears as an Apion boatman in P. Ox. 133. On these boatmen see pp. 78-79, 109-110, *infra*.

Corresponding items in the accounts of pronoetae would record the wheat for embolé and the money for naulage paid to the boatmen.[1] The payment of money taxes was still more indirect. The pronoetae turned over their net receipts to the estate cashier; [2] and the tax payments seem then to have been made for the estate as a whole.[3]

It seems probable that the Apion estate was responsible for collecting the taxes of others besides its own tenants. A group of items in the Apion accounts record payments on private land,[4] or on public land; [5] and one clearly mentions taxes on private land.[6] Probably these are cases of peasants who had come under the patronage of the Apion family, but had not surrendered all their rights. Hence they paid only taxes, and not rent, upon the land in question. Under the terms of the edict of 415, however, the government must have regarded such land as Apion property. The terms used, "private" and "public," may be an interesting but meaningless survival of the older classes of Egyptian land, which had otherwise died out in the fifth century.[7]

Probably somewhat different is the case in which we hear of an Apion employee collecting taxes from the villages of Mouchis and Pinuris.[8] Pinuris seems to have been Apion property, and the collection there may really have been of

[1] P. Ox. 1912, 120; 1913, 61-62; probably 1911, 76-77, an entry occupying the same place in the account as the payment for embolé in 1912. The only legible word is "to Cyriacus," the boatman mentioned in 1913.

[2] P. Ox. 1911, 212-217; 1912, 162-167; 1914, 6-14. P. Ox. 143 is a group of receipts for such payments.

[3] See pp. 55-57, *infra*.

[4] P. Ox. 1912, 87; 2037, 10, 30, 32.

[5] P. Ox. 2019, 20.

[6] PSI 954, 23.

[7] For which process see Bell, "Epoch in the Agrarian History of Egypt" in *Recueil Champollion*.

[8] P. Ox. 1855.

estate dues.[1] Taxes are clearly referred to at Mouchis. I suggest tentatively that some member of the Apion family was pagarch at the moment and used estate officials for public business. The line between an office-holder and the same man in his private capacity was always a very thin one in ancient times.

Autopragia first appears in a law of 383 providing that the staff of the provincial government was to collect the taxes of large landowners, decurions those of other members of the *curiae,* and the municipal defensors those of small proprietors.[2] The growth of the custom is shown by a law of 399 which states that many were demanding exemption from the regular system of collection and orders that no change is to be made in the customary manner of tax payment.[3] Similarly, a law of 409 decrees that the right of the so-called *autopractores* is to be abolished and all collections are to be made by the *curiales* unless a special grant of privilege is given.[4] In 429 the custom of autopragia received a partial recognition. The landowners of Africa were given four months to pay their taxes at the Capitol in Carthage *studio spontaneae devotionis.* If the taxes were not delivered by that time, they would be collected by the government.[5] The only reason why the subject of autopragia does not appear in the legislation of the sixth-century is that the institution was a thoroughly recognized one.[6]

[1] It is not clear what relation this collection had to the functions of the pronoetes of Pinuris, who appears in the same series, P. Ox. 1853.

[2] C. T. xi, 7 (12).

[3] C. T. xi, 7 (15).

[4] C. T. xi, 22 (4).

[5] C. T. xi, 1 (34), discussed by Matthias Gelzer "Zum αὐτόπρακτον σχῆμα der P. Aphrodito Cairo," in *Archiv.* v, pp. 188-189. Doubtless the concession was due to the disturbed state of Africa at the time.

[6] But Gelzer's "Im C. J. fehlen die Autopragieverbote, offenbar weil seither überall die Grossgrundbesitzer autoprakt geworden waren" in *Studien,* p. 89, goes somewhat beyond our evidence.

There is a possible reference to autopragia in the edict of 538 in the phrase, " the soldiers and pagarchs and those who administer the taxes which are under their direction (διοίκησις) and authority." [1] We see the institution most clearly, however, in the documents from Aphrodito. The village of Aphrodito claimed to have had, since the time of the emperor Leo, the right to pay its taxes according to the αὐτόπρακτον σχῆμα; [2] and it protested vigorously against the invasion of this right by successive pagarchs of Antaeopolis.[3] The privileges which it enjoyed are clear in the records. It paid its money taxes directly to the provincial administration of the Thebaid, its receipts for tax payments coming from the provincial treasurer.[4] For the embolé it received an order from the praeses directing it to load the grain in small boats and send it to Alexandria.[5] At least in the payment of imperial taxes it was, therefore, entirely independent of the officials of the pagarchy in which it was located.

The Apion family enjoyed the right of autopragia to an even fuller extent. Its money tax payments were sent direct to Alexandria, and so did not pass through the hands of either the officials of the pagarchy of Oxyrhynchus or those of the province of Arcadia. The main evidence for this is a group of references in the Apion documents. We hear of " the gold of the installment for Phaophi of the first indiction " [6] or " the second installment of the revenue " [7] going to

[1] Edict xiii, 12.

[2] P. Cairo 67019; 67002 iii, 8.

[3] P. Cairo 67283; 67019; 67024 (Julianus, c. 550-552); 67002 (Menas, c. 568). For the dating see Jean Maspero, " Les papyrus Beaugé," in the *Bulletin de l'institut francais d'archéologie orientale*, vol. x, pp. 131-157; pp. 137-143.

[4] P. Cairo 67033-67035; 67038; 67039; P. Lond. 1664.

[5] P. Cairo 67030; 67280; P. Flor. 292-293.

[6] P. Amherst 157.

[7] PSI 953, 68-69, 78-79.

Alexandria. The term used is the technical one referring to the three installments in which taxes were then paid.[1] A detachment of the military force of the estate was sent to guard the money on its way.[2] Different personages were sent on different occasions to carry the money. In Phaophi, 612, one of the estate cashiers went to Alexandria for this purpose.[3] A letter of the same period very probably refers to a special collector despatched on a similar errand. The letter, which is from one high estate official to another, reads as follows:

Immediately and at once let your true illustriousness send me here Theodore the παραπομπός, since the illustrious money-changer expects him to go down to Alexandria. By all means be sure to bring him with you and arrive quickly by the day after tomorrow, for, the Lord knows, I can't stand any longer the illustrious money-changer troubling me. So by all means come the day after tomorrow with the παραπομπός.[4]

A contract of 580, drawn up by whoever carried the money in that year, mentions the sum of 2160 solidi. This amount, which is exactly 30 pounds of gold, suggests a fixed annual assessment of 90 pounds; but unfortunately we do not know how much of the estate this covers and cannot say whether the tax was light or heavy. The document is worth quoting:

I have received from your magnificence through John, your most distinguished cashier, for the revenues of the third installment of the thirteenth indiction 1440 gold solidi in pure coin and 720 solidi in independent Egyptian coin, Alexandrian stand-

[1] C. J. x, 16 (13). *Cf.* Rouillard, *op. cit.*, p. 92.

[2] PSI 953, 68-69, 78-79.

[3] P. Amherst 157.

[4] P. Ox. 1844. Παραπομπός as a messenger delivering taxes occurs in P. Ox. 127; money changers receiving taxes at Alexandria in P. Ox. 127 and 144.

ard, with 45 solidi to make it up to purity, total 2205 gold solidi. This I am prepared to take to Alexandria, apart from act of God and dangers and accidents by river, and to deliver it to John and Simeon, the most illustrious money-changers, bringing a written receipt from the most illustrious apocrisarius [1] Theodore that the aforesaid sum of money has been paid in full.[2]

It seems probable that a similar privilege was enjoyed with regard to grain payments. The village of Aphrodito seems to have been responsible for the transportation of its embolé to Alexandria.[3] The Apion estate had more extensive privileges with regard to money taxes than did Aphrodito, and would scarcely have had lesser rights with regard to grain. Unfortunately there is no direct evidence as to just what the estate boatmen did with the grain they collected for embolé. The estate was in touch with embolators, presumably officials charged with collecting the embolé, but it is by no means certain that they had to do with the estate in their official capacity. The embolators figure most prominently in the accounts as purchasers of surplus grain. We hear of their receiving fees. But this payment was on the way to become a separate tax,[4] and it therefore does not prove other official contact with the embolators. A payment "for the second installment" perhaps refers to the part of the embolé which went to the church of Alexandria and was collected slightly later than the grain.[5] Until further evidence ap-

[1] Apocrisiarius is a perfectly colorless word meaning delegate. Probably it here refers to the palatine, delegate at Alexandria of the Count of the Sacred Largesses, Rouillard, *op. cit.*, p. 110. The monetary unit of the period was the solidus, 1/72 of a pound of gold, which was divided into 24 karats.

[2] P. Ox. 144.

[3] P. Cairo 67030; 67280. *Cf.* Gelzer "Altes und Neues," p. 376.

[4] P. Ox. 1911, 209; 1914, 5-6. Presumably the embolator was authorized to purchase grain for the embolé with money paid for that tax by *adaeratio*. *Cf.* P. Ox. 1999.

[5] P. Ox. 1908. *Cf.* Rouillard, *op. cit.*, pp. 139-140.

pears, the question must remain open. The case of Aphrodito will again show us that complete consistency did not prevail in these matters. Aphrodito sent its regular embolé to Alexandria, but handed over on the spot the part which was appropriated to the monastery of the Metanoia.[1]

It is sometimes assumed that the large landowners as a class were autopract;[2] it must be said, however, that this is, after all, an assumption. It is clearly evident that the Apion estate and the village of Aphrodito possessed the privilege of autopragia; and autopragia was certainly a recognized institution, if we may judge from the way in which the papyri talk about it. But the two other estates from which we have considerable evidence are at least not yet clearly proved autopract. In the four years covered by the account from the Hermopolis estate the tax items recur regularly as follows: (1) 113 artabae for taxes of Hermopolis,[3] (2) tax of Hermopolis, also called tax of the κτῆσις, paid through the ἀπαιτητὴς σιτικῶν, 108⅓ artabae,[4] (3) naulage of the artabae of grain, 25¼ karats,[5] (4) tax of the lady, tax of the κτῆσις, or tax of the κτῆσις of Hermopolis.[6] It appears from the arrangement of the account that these were all charges on one of the two sections of the estate. The other paid (5) tax of Pesla, 64⅙ artabae,[7] and (6) tax of Pesla, with houses of

[1] P. Cairo 67286; 67347.

[2] *E. g.*, Gelzer, *Studien*, p. 89; P. Cairo 67283, introduction; Rouillard, *op. cit.*, p. 202, etc.

[3] P. Bad. 95, 157, 436, 477. The same item is probably to be restored earlier in the record of the 8th indiction.

[4] P Bad. 95, 56 (as restored by Schnebel, "Agricultural Ledger," p. 38), 159, 437, 478.

[5] P. Bad. 95, 86, 191, 448, 495.

[6] P. Bad. 95, 84, 189, 447.

[7] P. Bad. 95, 158, 280, 346, and to be restored in the record of the 8th indiction, along with (1) and (2).

the village, 6 solidi, 8 karats.[1] Items (5) and (6) are obviously the embolé and money tax on the part of the estate which lay in the village of Pesla,[2] nor is there any indication that they were paid otherwise than through the village authorities. Items (1) and (2) are payments of embolé on the part of the estate lying within the collecting area of the city of Hermopolis. The ἀπαιτητής mentioned in this connection was a municipal tax-collecting official.[3] Items (3) and (4) likewise were probably paid to the local authorities.

The situation on the estate of Count Ammonius is similar. His lands were included in the codex drawn up by John, scholasticus and censitor, which seems to have been the official register of taxable lands at Aphrodito.[4] His grain taxes were part of the embolé of Aphrodito, from which we may probably conclude that his other tax payments were part of the taxes of the village.[5] A lesser form of autopragia is indicated, however, by the receipts for grain from Count Ammonius' property delivered to the boat of the Metanoia. The grain was handed over directly by Count Ammonius' steward, but was credited as part of the embolé of Aphrodito or of the city taxes of Antaeopolis.[6] A few receipts acknowledge the payment of embolé to village officials by persons apparently of considerably greater dignity.[7] These are perhaps further cases of non-autopract large landowners.

There seems to be some evidence that the landowners took

[1] P. Bad. 95, 85, 190, 299, 365.

[2] For an earlier reference to this village see P. Leipzig 54.

[3] *Cf.* Rouillard, *op. cit.*, pp. 116, 132-133.

[4] P. Cairo 67040 (full text, as printed in vol. iii). For the codex of John see P. Cairo 67097, R 41; 67117, 14; 67118, 30-31; 67329, 5; Rouillard, *op. cit.*, p. 130.

[5] P. Cairo 67139, vi R; 67138 ii V, iii R.

[6] P. Cairo 67138, iv R; 67347.

[7] P. Klein, Form. 95; 356.

over government functions in the sphere of irrigation. It is not, of course, remarkable that a large agricultural establishment should see to it that it received accurate reports of the beginning of the inundation,[1] or that estate officials should have occasion to busy themselves with the measuring of uninundated and unsown land.[2] We are not surprised to find the Apion estate building dikes, or even repairing a watercourse called "the governor's canal."[3] There seems to be something new, however, in an account of work done on the dikes of Tarousebt, part of the Apion estate.[4] On the verso is an account of the receipts of the dike superintendent (χωματεπείκτης) with the note that part had been used for his pay and other expenses, part transferred to the estate account. As some of the places mentioned as contributing to this fund were Apion property and others were not, it looks as if the Apion estate had assumed the care of the dikes for a certain district, collecting money for the purpose.[5] It is certainly rather curious that, up to the present, little trace has been found of public work on the dikes in Byzantine Egypt.[6] The private enterprise of landowners may well have had to fill the gap.

The existence of bands of soldiers under the control of private individuals and acting in their interest is one of the

[1] P. Ox. 1830.

[2] P. Ox. 1842.

[3] P. Ox. 2035. On private dams *cf.* Michael Schnebel, *Die Landwirtschaft im hellenistischen Ägypten*, vol. i, in *Münchener Beiträge zur Papyrusforschung und antiken Rechtsgeschichte*, hft. 7, Munich, 1925, p 38.

[4] P. Ox. 1053. Tarousebt appears as Apion property in P. Ox. 1911.

[5] This perhaps explains the item in another account "from the protocometae of Taamorus for the canal constructed from the east of Pselemachis" (P. Ox. 1917, 111).

[6] The one exception, as far as I know, is P. Hamburg 56 (Paul M. Meyer, *Griechische Papyrusurkunden der Hamburger Staats-und Universitätsbibliothek*, Leipzig, 1924).

most remarkable new features in Byzantine Egypt. From the military bread, *bucella,* these soldiers derived the name of *bucellarii,* as we say "doughboys." They fall into two classes. Those who were in the service of the higher military commanders formed an important part of the armies of the sixth century. We are concerned here, however, with the second group, the *bucellarii* employed by private landowners.[1] The earliest mention of these private *bucellarii* is in a law of the Emperor Leo, dating from 468: "we wish the right to keep *bucellarii* or Isaurians and armed slaves to be abolished in all cities and country places. If anyone, contrary to this beneficent decree of serenity, attempts to keep armed servants or *bucellarii* or Isaurians on his estate or about himself" he is to be fined one hundred pounds of gold, and governors who fail to enforce the law are threatened with even severer penalties.[2] The ineffectiveness of this law is shown by one of Justinian seventy years later in which, describing the conditions which he hoped to meet by a stronger government in Cappadocia, he says, "for those who administer the estates of the wealthy,—but we blush even to state how brazenly they act and how δορύφοροι [the regular expression for the higher grade among the bucellarii maintained by military commanders] serve them and an unbearable multitude of men follow them and they shamelessly rob everybody."[3]

Both types of *bucellarii* are found in Egypt. Official *bucellarii* appear at Oxyrhynchus in the service of the *praeses* of Arcadia. They come there under the tribune Oulior, apparently for the suppression of some disturbance.[4]

[1] *Cf.* on the whole subject Robert Grosse, *Römische Militärgeschichte von Gallienus bis zum Beginn der byzantinischen Themenverfassung,* Berlin, 1920, pp. 283-291.

[2] C. J. ix, 12 (10).

[3] Nov. 30 (5).

[4] P. Ox. 1888 and 2046 (with which 1903 overlaps); 2046, 56 "Macarius, slave, going to Heracleopolis after the proclamations of suppression of violence."

Of the private *bucellarii* there are many traces. Among those who are known to have employed them are the Apion family, several proprietors in the Fayum,[1] the church of Hermopolis,[2] and Count Ammonius.[3]

One of the Apion documents refers to the appointment of *bucellarii*. The landlord's agent Theodore addresses a letter to the chartularii and μειζότεροι of the estate, as follows:

Please enroll the bearers, Abraham and Nicetas, *bucellarii*, from the beginning of Pharmouthi and give them their allowances in kind, since you know that we need *bucellarii*; please do this without delay.[4]

The officials addressed were apparently those in charge of the accounting and the supplies of the estate.[5] The "enrolling" of these *bucellarii* probably meant listing them for pay. The pay of *bucellarii* presumably included allowances of bread, meat, oil, and wine, such as were regularly given to soldiers in this period.[6] The *bucellarii* of the Apion family received meat at the rate of one pound a day,[7] which is the standard rate in contemporary military accounts. Their wine allowance was probably at the rate of one quarter of a double measure, which again corresponds to the pay of soldiers.[8] From some similar establishment comes an order for

[1] P. Klein Form. 344; 1093.

[2] P. Lond. 1776; 1783.

[3] P. Cairo 67062.

[4] P. Ox. 156; P. Klein Form. 1093 also seems to refer to the installation of a *bucellarius*.

[5] See pp. 94-95, 104-105, *infra*.

[6] Allowances to soldiers and official *bucellarii* in P. Ox. 1888; 1903; 1920; and 2046.

[7] P. Ox. 2013; 2014.

[8] PSI 953, 29, one man for a month 7½ διπλᾶ; 33, two men for 16 days, 8 διπλᾶ; 35, three men "Pharmouthi 23-30, 28 days, 21 διπλᾶ."—but as 23-30 is not 28 days, κγ was probably a slip for γ; 43-44, two men 15

the issue of oil to *bucellarii*.[1] An Apion account indicates that they were also paid in money.[2]

Many of the official *bucellarii* whose names are preserved were evidently foreigners. One account, for instance, mentions Tancila, Ilderich, Boraides and Zemarchus the Bessians, and John and Sambas of Salonae.[3] The Gothic slaves whom the Apion estate maintained with their families were perhaps used in this capacity.[4] The equipment of *bucellarii* included at least swords and shields, as we see from a letter in which an agent of Count Ammonius is directed to collect two solidi which were owing to him, sending one on to pay for a sword which had been given to the soldier Stephen,[5] and from an incidental reference in one of the Apion documents.[6]

The Apion document just cited is a letter in which some estate official addresses the pronoetes of Parkerke as follows:

> Send me at once today John and Parsacis with their swords and shields, as I wish them with me. Be sure to send them today.

This would suggest that some, at least, of the *bucellarii* were scattered over the estate in small detachments. This is perhaps confirmed by the small groups, never more than thirteen, which appear as receiving provisions. The one exception is an item in an Apion wine account:

> to the *bucellarii* attending on the glorious house, expenses of

days, 3½ διπλᾶ,—but the γ is marked as doubtful and should perhaps be read ζ; P. Ox. 150, 14 men 1 day, 3½ διπλᾶ. The soldiers in 1920 are given two sextarii on an 8-sextarius διπλοῦν.

[1] BGU 963.

[2] PSI 953, 18.

[3] P. Ox. 1903.

[4] PSI 953, 17, 32, 47, 84-85; 956, 26.

[5] P. Cairo 67062.

[6] P. Ox. 1839; the provision of shield-bosses for the Apion estate is mentioned in P. Ox. 1940.

Pauni, as in the schedule of the expenses of the first indiction, 302½ δ̇ιπλᾱ.[1]

At the rate prevailing elsewhere this would cover 40 bucellarii for the whole month and one for ten days, or some such combination.[2] This unusually phrased item perhaps gives us the total number of *bucellarii* on the Apion estate, at least in the Oxyrhynchus area. We gather that *bucellarii* from the Cynopolite and Heracleopolite nomes were sent from time to time to help the estate forces at Oxyrhynchus.[3]

To the *bucellarii* must be added certain other employees who at least might be armed. Messengers (σύμμαχοι) are mentioned in one of the Apion documents as *spatharii* (swordsmen).[4] A petition from Oxyrhynchus refers to messengers actually taking part in an armed attack.[5] On the other hand, the local field guards (ἀγροφύλακες) do not seem to be in quite the same position. Their relation to villages was apparently half way between that of village officials and that of a hereditary professional group.[6] An estate might sometimes compensate them for guarding its property,[7] but more often it would come in contact with them merely as coloni. Our records provide cases of estates collecting rent from field guards,[8] throwing them into an estate prison,[9] or taking surety against their leaving the land.[10]

1 PSI 953, 48-49.

2 See *supra*, p. 62.

3 PSI 953, 41; P. Ox. 150.

4 P. Ox. 2045. Two of the messengers there mentioned appear in P. Ox. 2057 as possessors of shields.

5 PSI 872.

6 P. Cairo 67001 and 67328 illustrate the relation between the village of Aphrodito and its field guards.

7 *E. g.*, P. Ox. 141; 1913, 16-18; PSI 165; 954, 55.

8 P. Bad. 95, 40, 419.

9 P. Ox. 2056.

10 P. Lond. 778.

The only legitimate use of *bucellarii* would have been as watchmen, such as we find on estates long before the Byzantine period.[1] Our evidence certainly suggests, however, that the habits of *bucellarii* in Egypt were not so different from those Justinian complained of in Cappadocia. Occasionally, to be sure, these private forces seemed to have filled the gap left by the inefficiency of the government. Such a situation appears in a letter addressed to Leontius, a landowner in the Oxyrhynchite nome. The writer reports that a distressing fight recently took place at Sinaru which would have depopulated that village but for divine providence and the intervention of the *liturgi*; and he asks Leontius to meet the situation by sending two messengers.[2] The church recognized some responsibility for doing what it could when the barbarians broke in from the south. The great White Monastery with its massive walls and extensive resources was, at least once, able to protect and feed a large body of refugees.[3] A fifth-century bishop of Syene petitioned the emperor that the soldiers at Syene be instructed to cooperate with him, apparently even to obey his orders, complaining that his church had been unable to protect its own fugitives.[4]

The usual business of *bucellarii,* however, was the vindication of real or alleged private rights. Victor, soldier of the church of Hermopolis, for instance, collected debts due to that institution.[5] The way the general public felt about the activities of both official and private *bucellarii* appears quite

[1] M. Rostowzew, "Die Domänenpolizei in dem römischen Kaiserreiche" in *Philologus,* vol. 64 (Neue Folge, vol. 18), 1905, pp. 297-307.

[2] PSI 71; the *liturgi* would be the body of liturgical village officials.

[3] Johannes Leipoldt, *Schenute von Atripe und die Entstehung des national ägyptischen Christentums* in C. v. Gebhardt and A. Harnack, *Texte und Untersuchungen zur Geschichte der altchristlichen Literatur,* vol. xv, 1, Leipzig, 1903, pp. 171-173.

[4] P. Leid. Z., republished in Wilcken, *Chrestomathie,* as No. 6.

[5] P. Lond. 1776.

clearly in a petition addressed to a new duke of the Thebaid. After speaking of the blessings which are expected from his rule it adds:

May your grace also protect us against the following: namely, the so-called *bucellarii* who go through the country illegally taking their own pay in a disorderly manner and treating as their profit what others have worked for, and those who let their armed servants act as they will, rather increasing than decreasing the sufferings of the landowners.[1]

A specific complaint is preserved in a petition from Oxyrhynchus in which the petitioner asks for the voiding of an agreement which a certain Philoxenus had forced from him by introducing " barbarian slaves, servants, and messengers " into his house.[2]

Perhaps the most significant document of all is a petition addressed to the civil governor of Arcadia by the officers of the devoted Transtigritani, one of the detachments stationed at Arsinoë. A few days before they had sent soldiers to collect the grain allowance which they regularly received from the village of Kerke. The villagers drove them away, but later asked for pardon, saying they had been under compulsion, the *bucellarii* of a certain patrician having demanded heavy payments from them without right. The petition continues:

and we call on your honor and implore you by the Lord Christ . . . and our most pious and victorious Lord Flavius Justinian, eternal Augustus and emperor, to order the dioecetae of that glorious house . . . [to restrain the] *bucellarii*, who have no authority in the said village, so that there may be no opposition

[1] P. Cairo 67089 R 12-16.

[2] PSI 872. There is a hint of something which would be interesting, if we knew the details, in P. Ox. 150, an Apion document recording the issue of wine " to the fourteen *bucellarii* of Heracleopolis and Coma who came here on account of the fight." *Cf.* P. Flor. 295.

from these *bucellarii* to our soldiers when they go for our *annonae*, as above mentioned, and the proper harmony may prevail.[1]

Presumably there was some claim behind the actions described in the two documents last quoted. It should be remembered that such procedure in defense of private rights was not wholly unlike contemporary methods of law enforcement. A letter is extant in which the riparius of Oxyrhynchus threatens certain local officials that if they do not immediately arrest the men who are ravaging the fields he will have the tribune send soldiers to plunder their houses,—not the whole village but their particular houses.[2] Similarly we read in an account of a rebellion that the first overt act of the three brothers who led it, apparently themselves members of the landowning and office-holding class, was the sacking of a town " without the authorization of the prefect of the nome." [3] Apparently with his authorization it would have been all right.

Another symptom of the way in which powerful individuals took the law into their own hands is the existence of private prisons, which are known both from laws against them and from references to their operation. The fact that two out of the three laws on the subject are connected with Egypt seems to imply that the institution was particularly developed in that country. Private prisons first appear in the late fourth century, the time when the large estates of Byzantine Egypt were first being built up. In 388 Theodo-

[1] BGU 836, accepting the readings proposed by Maspero, *Organisation militaire*, pp. 75-76, and addenda to p. 75. The patrician referred to is not impossibly a member of the Apion family.

[2] PSI 47.

[3] John of Nikou, *Chronicle*, 97 (M. H. Zotenberg, *Chronique de Jean, évêque de Nikiou*, in *Notices et extraits des manuscrits de la bibliothèque nationale*, vol. 24, Paris, 1883).

sius I wrote briefly in an edict addressed to the augustal prefect of Egypt: " Let anyone who hereafter confines a criminal in a private prison be held guilty of *maiestas*." [1] Almost a century later, in 486, Zeno found it necessary to decree

that no one in the city of Alexandria or the diocese of Egypt or any province of our empire be allowed to maintain a private prison either on his estate or anywhere.

The augustal prefect and governors generally were threatened with the severest penalties if they neglected the enforcement of this law.[2] Yet in 529 Justinian is forced again to order, " we forbid private prisons to exist anywhere in cities or villages " providing the interesting penalty that violators are to stay as long in the public jail as any one had been kept in their private prisons and are to lose any case they may have against such persons. The emperor Zeno's threats of confiscation and death for negligent governors are repeated.[3]

There is a possible reference to a private prison in a petition of about 465 in which a peasant complains that he had been unjustly imprisoned by one of the decurions of Cynopolis, although he was ready to pay any debt that could be proved in writing.[4] In the next century we see these prisons, which the emperors so strictly and ineffectively prohibited, in regular operation. The estate prison on the Apion estate was apparently a quite normal part of the establishment. We have records of the wine which the prisoners, as in public prisons, received on festivals,—Easter, Epiphany, and St. Michael's day happen to be referred to. On the last-named holiday in the year from which our in-

[1] C. T. ix, 11 (1).
[2] C. J. ix, 5 (1).
[3] C. J. ix, 5 (2).
[4] P. Ox. 902.

formation comes, perhaps 538, there were 139 persons in the estate prison.[1]

Our information as to just how estate prisons were used is unfortunately not complete. At least on the Apion estate it was at the estate prison that the fugitive colonus was to be produced by his surety.[2] In other cases the estate prison seems to be used somewhat, as it were, informally, as a means of putting pressure on individuals or villages. Thus, at least according to a subsequent complaint, it was to force her to give up her rights that a peasant woman in the Thebaid was placed by a local landowner "ἐν τῇ ἰδικῇ αὐτοῦ φυλακῇ."[3] A sixth-century letter informs us of a possible use of the institution:

The bearer stated that you were detaining his wife in prison and had seized his property. Please release the property, keeping the wife until he produces what he owes.[4]

Two documents, quite possibly from the Apion estate, show us the same procedure applied to a whole village through its notables. One is a "list of the persons from Teruthis thrown into the prison of the house of Anianus," among whom were a headman and ex-headman, four guards, a priest, and an oeconomus.[5] The other is a letter in which

[1] PSI 953, 37, 54-60; for issue of wine to public prisons, *cf.* P. Ox. 1945.

[2] The phrase is "in the φυλακῇ of your glorious house" (P. Ox. 135; PSI 61; 62; for φυλακή as "prison" *cf.* Preisigke, *Wörterbuch*, s. v). A comparison with contemporary documents makes the meaning clear. Bonds of surety at the corresponding point promise that the person will be produced in a public place, P. Strassburg, 46-51 (Friedrich Preisigke, *Griechische Papyrus der kaiserlichen Universitäts- und Landesbibliothek zu Strassburg*, Leipzig, 1912-1920 2 vols.); P. Cairo 67296-67297; 67328, or at a public prison (BGU 255; PSI 52). P. Ox. 135 speaks of both the public place and the estate prison; probably the notary confused the two forms.

[3] P. Cairo 67005, 18.

[4] PSI 824.

[5] P. Ox. 2056. Teruthis appears in Apion documents and a field "of Gedius Anianus" (P. Ox. 137); *cf.* p. 134, *infra.*

Phoebammon and Phib urge the diocetes Maiamacis to release the wives of the protocometae, seven in number, assuring him that they will bring them to prison whenever directed to do so.[1] Neither document, unfortunately, gives us any statement of the reason why the action was taken. We are surely justified, however, in concluding that the village as a whole was being reached through its chief inhabitants.

Some kind of formality, if no more than the issuing of an order, must have accompanied the committing of a person to the estate prison. While this does not give us the right to talk about private criminal jurisdiction, at least occasionally estate prisons served for the confinement of criminals. The Apion estate seems also to have had some responsibility for apprehending such criminals. In one Apion papyrus a list of coloni who had fled the estate is followed by these notes:

> About the murderer from Leon who is with the people of Philostratus.
> About Pasoein of Leon who is in Philostratus.
> About Asyrius of Leon who is in Philostratus.
> About Pathone of Peles who stole the oxen of Diogenes and is in the κτῆμα of Machauson.
> About the people of Calybe, also those of Atha [ ?] who took eight loads of bricks.[2]

Theft and murder and the escape of serfs are mixed up together as matters of estate concern. A document headed "list of those shut up in the prison, Mesore 14" [3] is probably a report from a private prison. The first case is one of two peasants who were arrested by the landlord's agent for sheep stealing. In the four other cases mentioned the offi-

[1] P. Ox. 1835. The title "dioecetes" points either to the Apion estate or to some similar establishment.

[2] P. Ox. 2055.

[3] P. Stud. Pal. x, 252; photograph published in Rouillard, *op. cit.*, p. 155.

cial who makes the arrest is once the defensor, twice the riparius, once Count George, chartularius.[1] The defensor was, of course, a municipal official, while the landlord's agent would be a private employee and the others might also be such. It seems hard to say whether we have here the state sending its prisoners to a private lock-up, or an influential magnate who is allowed to commit men to the public jail. One of the cases incidentally illustrates the sometimes rough and ready methods of Byzantine justice,—" Anna, wife of Phib, goat-butcher, arrested because her brother stole the messenger's money."

The riparius here mentioned may have been, as riparii usually are, a police official; but he may also have been in private service. The maintenance of riparii was sometimes entrusted to the landowners. Thus a group of proprietors shared the responsibility for the riparii of the house of Theon, probably, as suggested above, a section of the Oxyrhynchite nome.[2] This in itself was only a development of the liturgical system; but at Heracleopolis we hear of a " riparius of the glorious house of Apion." [3] At Oxyrhynchus riparii appear among those connected with the estate; but whether they were employees or village riparii in the sphere of influence of the Apion estate is hard to determine.[4] At least an unofficial private exercise of police functions appears in a letter from the Apion series. The landlord's agent Victor informs a subordinate estate official that he is sending to him several witnesses of the attack which the people of Thmoinepsobthis have recently made on Pinuris, which seems to have been part of the Apion property. The imperial official (δεσποτικός) has sent for the headmen of Thmoinep-

[1] On chartularii, *infra*, pp. 94-95.

[2] P. Ox. 2039. *Cf. supra*, pp. 47-49.

[3] P. Klein. Form. 86.

[4] P. Ox. 1854; 2032, 50.

sobthis, and apparently some kind of joint hearing is to be held in the hope of completing the investigation and recovering the stolen money.[1] The Apion estate and, apparently, the imperial estate administration, are here cooperating in what is essentially a criminal investigation. Unfortunately, it is not clear by what authority they were acting.

It was quite common at this period to substitute an informal hearing before agreed arbitrators for a judicial trial, or at least to attempt such a hearing.[2] It is perhaps merely as an imposing arbitrator that the Apion estate sometimes interfered in disputes; even this is a quasi-judicial action. Thus it was that the pronoetes of Pakerke was instructed:

> Cause Cyriacus the son of Bamus to come to arbitration with the woman who brings this letter. Be sure to cause him to do so. As the Lord lives if she comes to me again and they are not reconciled, you will not be able to endure my wrath.[3]

Similarly, the landlord's agent wrote to one of the dioecetae of the estate, directing him to see to the carrying out of an agreement relating to a division of property, perhaps between heirs.[4] A similar situation on ecclesiastical property is reflected in a letter addressed to an archimandrite, in which the writer urges him to see that a certain quarrel was settled "according to justice and the custom of the κτῆμα."[5]

An estate might take a hand in disputes between villages as well as in the disagreements of individuals. Such is the case, probably, on the Apion estate in which we hear of a dioecetes recommending preliminary negotiations with reference to cattle which one village had taken from another,

[1] P. Ox. 1853.

[2] *E. g.*, P. Lond. 113, 1.

[3] P. Ox. 1839.

[4] P. Ox. 1847.

[5] BGU 103. The archimandrite-landlord is apparently asked to prevent a lawsuit by bringing about such a settlement.

" so that when our master, the landlord's agent, who is with you, arrives they may jointly reconcile us." [1] Several interpretations are possible for a document in which a local official agrees on behalf of the people of Popano to pay 18 solidi to the Apion estate " by reason of the charge of damage at Parkerke by the people of Popano." The phrase translated " by reason of the charge of damage " is ὑπὲρ τοῦ ἀναιρεθέντος which could also be translated " on account of the man who was murdered." [2] We are probably justified in seeing in this case the prestige of the Apion estate securing the favorable settlement out of court of a cause of dispute, whatever the cause was.

Landowners seem to have had some influence on the weights and measures used in Byzantine Egypt. The country suffered from great confusion as to standards. Several different standards of gold coinage appear. The Alexandrian standard differed from the imperial solidus,[3] and not only nome-capitals but even villages had their own local standards.[4] The attempt of Justinian in 559 to suppress all

[1] P. Ox. 1867. It is not impossible that the chief messenger of Mescanounis, who in P. Ox. 1866 is mentioned as the proper person to preside over the return of property stolen from one village by another, was an Apion rather than a village employee. Mescanounis is elsewhere (P. Ox. 1915; 2032, 22) part of the Apion estate.

[2] P. Ox. 1897.

[3] Public and Alexandrian standards in Oxyrhynchus Papyri of the period *passim*. Edict xi and P. Ox. 144 give the premium in 559 and 580 for good money over independent Egyptian coinage (9 and 4½ solidi, respectively, in the pound of 72 solidi).

[4] P. Munich 1 (August Heisenberg and Leopold Wenger, *Byzantinische Papyri in der Königlichen Hof-und Staatsbibliothek zu München*, Leipzig, 1914), note to line 53, lists standards of Arsinoë, Hermopolis, Antaeopolis, Syene, and a village in the Hermopolite nome. To this should be added the standard of Spania in the Oxyrhynichite (PSI 77). The condition seems to get worse in the south,—at Oxyrhynchus we only see slight variations in weight, at Aphrodito a solidus of 22 karats instead of the standard 24 (P. Cairo, 67138 intro. p. 26).

money except the official imperial coinage was, as might have been expected, a failure.[1] The private standard which we hear of has been explained as the standard of private proprietors.[2] The suggestion, however, seems improbable. The private standard occurs only in documents from Oxyrhynchus, and Oxyrhynchus is the only nome-capital for which we have a number of documents of the Byzantine period with no reference to a local standard. Very probably, therefore, the standard which is called private in Oxyrhynchus documents is actually the local Oxyrhynchite standard, thus distinguished from the public and Alexandrian standards.[3]

When standards were so confused, gold coins would, of course, often be weighed rather than counted. Ordinary creditors could insist on having money paid by specified scales,[4] and we need scarcely doubt that large estates would do the same. A number of bronze coins of the 5th century have been preserved which are careful reproductions of official coinages, but are on a reduced scale, and therefore clearly more than mere attempts at forgery. It is not impossible that they were struck, as has been suggested, on private estates.[5]

The measures used for grain were in as confused a condition as the weights used for money. Hence it is not surprising that landlords insisted on their own artaba-basket being used to measure the grain they received.[6] Sometimes

[1] Edict xi, on which see Charles Diehl, *Une crise monetaire au VI^e siècle*, in *Revue des Etudes Grecques*, vol. xxxii, 1919, pp. 158-166.

[2] P. Munich, 1, note to line 53.

[3] For the three together see *e. g.*, P. Ox. 1918 R i.

[4] P. Grenfell ii, 90.

[5] J. G. Milne, "The Currency of Egypt in the Fifth Century," in the *Numismatic Chronicle*, Series v. vol. vi, 1926, pp. 43-92, and "Feudal Currency in Roman Egypt," in *Ancient Egypt*, March, 1926, pp. 5-9.

[6] PSI 283; P. Ox. 136, 27-29; P. Lond. 1001; P. Flor. 281.

it would seem that a landowner set up a distinct measure of his own. An account from Aphrodito distinguishes two payments of grain as " by our measure " and " by the measure of Antaeopolis." [1] The measure of Count Ammonius seems to have been used by others in his neighborhood. At least, payment of grain by the measure of Count Ammonius is specified once in a lease not connected with his estate.[2]

The system of serfdom presents a somewhat less complicated picture than the feudal or quasi-feudal phenomena with which the first part of this chapter has been concerned. The colonate was an accepted part of the social system of the sixth century. The phrase ἐναπόγραφος γεωργός, which is the Greek for *colonus adscripiticius*,[3] occurs frequently in bonds and other formal documents addressed to the Apion estate when the person concerned was of that class.[4] We also meet it in a document from the property of the church of Oxyrhynchus,[5] and probably it is only the absence of similar documents from other estates at Oxyrhynchus and elsewhere which prevents us from finding the exact phrase more often.

The fundamental fact about the condition of coloni was that they were bound to the soil. The laws of the time enshrined this in such phrases as " although admittedly free, yet they are treated as slaves of the land where they were born," [6] or " they are so closely bound to the soil that they

[1] P. Cairo 67141, iv, 18-19.

[2] P. Cairo 67300. The " measure of Dioscorides " in P. Strassburg 1 is perhaps something similar with regard to wine measures.

[3] C. J. xi, 48 (9).

[4] The phrase occurs in bonds of surety for coloni (P. Ox. 135; 200; 996; 1979; P. Lond. 778; PSI 61-2; 180), receipts for machinery (P. Ox. 137; 1982-1983; 1985; 1998-1991; P. Lond. 775), loans (P. Amherst 149), and promises to pay dues (P. Ox. 1896).

[5] P. Ox. 1900.

[6] C. J. xi, 52. The laws are summarized in Roth Clausing, *The Roman Colonate*, New York, 1925, Chap. i.

ought not to be separated even for an instant." [1] A feature which no law mentions is the precaution which was taken in Egypt, or at least at Oxyrhynchus, of having the coloni provided with sureties who would compensate the estate in case they did leave. A number of these bonds of surety are preserved. With the exception of two early documents which may be of this class [2] all come from the Apion estate. One example will illustrate the rather interesting standard form which they all follow:

To the most magnificent heirs of the late patrician Apion of glorious memory. . . . Aurelius Pamouthius, lead worker, son of George and Anniane, of the city of Oxyrhynchus. I voluntarily agree, taking the oath by God and the emperor, to be surety and pledge to your magnificence through your representatives for Aurelius Abraham, son of Herminus and Herais, a *colonus adscripticius* of yours, of the κτῆμα Great Tarouthinus, which belongs to your magnificence, in the Oxyrhynchite nome. I promise that he will continuously remain and reside in his κτῆμα with his family and wife and cattle and all his property, meeting all obligations resting on him personally or because of the position of *adscripticius*; and that he will in no way leave that same κτῆμα or move to another place. Moreover, if your magnificence through your representatives demands him of me at any time for any reason I will deliver him and hand him over in a public place without [regard for] any place of refuge or excuse as he was when I gave surety for him, in the prison of the same glorious house. If I do not do this I agree to forfeit for his disappearance and my failure to produce him eight gold solidi, actual payment of which is to be enforced.[3]

Although the actual precaution taken is not mentioned in the code, it is obviously in accordance with the spirit of their regulations on the colonate.

[1] C. J. xi, 48 (15).

[2] P. Stud. Pal. xx, 127 (Heracleopolis, 463 A. D.) and P. Lond. 1793 (Hermopolis, 472 A. D.).

[3] P. Ox. 135. On the form see see *supra*, p. 69.

Surety documents such as that given above confirm the suspicion which the laws give us that an attempt of coloni to leave an estate was by no means a remote possibility. A few actual cases have left records behind them. We perhaps have one in a letter in which the writer promises that if Apanacius comes back from the ἐποίκιον of Menas, the chief physician, neither he nor the field guard will be asked any question about the damage to the field.[1] Others are recorded in a "list of coloni who have fled from the κτῆμα of Thaesis to the κτῆμα of Machauson, belonging to the divine house."[2] Three escaped coloni from Leon, another Apion property, are mentioned in a group of supplementary notes appearing at the end of the document.[3] Twenty-three men of Thaesis are mentioned in the list. The flight of such a large group suggests something parallel to the peasants' strikes of the Ptolemaic period. In contrast, however, to the flight to a temple, characteristic of the earlier strikes, coloni who left their homes seem usually to have been able to find protection with other proprietors. The document just cited and imperial laws agree in describing the passage of coloni from one estate to another.[4] The form of surety, however, seems to be so phrased as to cover the possibility of their seeking the asylum of the church, the τόπος προσφυγῆς and λόγοι mentioned being a part of the institution of asylum.[5] Other surety bonds of the same period refer more explicitly to this right of sanctuary.[6]

[1] P. Lond. 1032.

[2] P. Ox. 2055.

[3] Thaesis is mentioned in P. Ox. 1910 V, Leon in P. Ox. 142-143; 1896, etc.

[4] *E. g.*, C. J. xi, 51.

[5] On asylum in this period see Friedrich von Woess, *Das Asylwesen Ägyptens in der Ptolemäerzeit und die spatere Entwicklung*, in *Münchener Beiträge zur Papyrusforschung und antiken Rechtsgeschichte*, hft. 5, Munich, 1923, pp. 229-237; on λόγοι, *cf.* Edict. xiii, 10, 28, etc.

[6] P. Strassburg 46-51; BGU 255; P. Cairo 67296; 67297; 67328.

We may notice several points in which the Apion documents coincide with what we know from other sources about the coloni. In the laws we find phrases like "their old homes in which they are registered and where they were born and brought up."[1] Similar expressions in the Apion papyri indicate the permanence of the relation. We are told: "I serve my good master as my fathers and forefathers did";[2] or again, "[we] have been, from our father and forefathers, living in the above-mentioned estate."[3] Coloni were forbidden to alienate their personal property without the lord's consent.[4] Surety bonds of the Apion group echo this provision. A special law prescribed that, although coloni were not allowed to take holy orders without their lord's consent, they might hold the priesthood in their own village while still being subject to the obligations of their position.[5] The Apion documents present two cases in which members of the clergy are definitely stated to be coloni.[6]

As is well known, the agricultural colonate was by no means the only form of hereditary status in the Byzantine system. In some cases regulation and in others custom kept a number of classes in the same position from father to son. Such hereditary groups are apparently mentioned in a petition from the Thebaid in which a number of plasterers, bronze workers, and carpenters say "from our fathers and forefathers we have had no other occupation than the practice of these trades."[7] Whether compulsory or not, the po-

[1] C. J. xi, 48 (6); note also the expression used in reference to the colonate, *aeternitatis iure*, C. J. xi, 51.

[2] P. Ox. 130.

[3] PSI 58.

[4] C. T. v. 19 (1); C. J. xi, 50 (2).

[5] C. J. i, 3 (16).

[6] P. Ox. 996; P. Lond. 778.

[7] P. Cairo 67020.

sition of boatman to the Apion estate seems to have been hereditary. We can trace one family of boatmen for at least three generations,—Asclas,[1] Menas, son of Asclas,[2] and "the heirs of the late Menas, son of Asclas captain of a boat of your glorious house."[3] Phib, son of Menas, and another Asclas, who appear as boatmen in documents probably earlier than those just cited,[4] perhaps carry the family back another generation or two.

Are we justified in drawing any general conclusion from these various semi-feudal phenomena? Perhaps the safest thing at present would be to say that many features of the feudal and manorial systems were present in Egypt in the last days of the Roman empire. But it is obviously unjustifiable to write as if either of these systems were present in its full development.

[1] P. Ox. 142 (534 A. D.).

[2] P. Ox. 1916, 39; 1998.

[3] P. Ox. 133 (550 A. D.).

[4] Phib in P. Ox. 1947-1948, Asclas in 1071 and 1929.

# CHAPTER V

## Estate Management

Large landowners at all periods have entrusted to others the actual work of running their property. Fourth century documents frequently contain the statement that a contract with a landowner has actually been made with his representatives.[1] Similar phrases occur quite frequently in the Apion papyri,—" the representatives of your magnificence entrusted the stable to me," [2] " I asked your magnificence through your representatives," [3] or " I promise your magnificence through your representatives." [4]

Of the Greek works to designate the estate managers which are used in the Byzantine period, ἀντιγεοῦχος, landlord's agent, is self-explanatory.[5] Dioecetes is quite commonly used both on private and on ecclesiastical estates.[6] Having no official use at this period, the word was apparently used purely with its etymological meaning in mind. διοικητὴς πραγμάτων of somebody occurs twice,[7] and a fifth century ad-

[1] P. Ox. 102 (306 A. D.); 103 (316 A. D.), the landowners concerned are in one case the daughter of an archon of Alexandria, in the other a prytanis of Oxyrhynchus.

[2] P. Ox. 138.

[3] *E. g.*, P. Ox. 1983.

[4] *E. g.*, P. Ox. 139.

[5] *E. g.*, BGU 303; 693; P. Klein Form. 1315.

[6] Private dioecetae, P. Ox. 1038; 1899; P. Klein Form. 1132. Ecclesiastical dioecetae, P. Cairo 67021 V, 16; 67151, 147; P. Flor. 377.

[7] P. Ox. 1899; P. Cairo 67151, 147.

ministrator of the imperial domain at Oxyrhynchus uses the title διοικῶν τὰ πράγματα and speaks of his διοίκησις.[1]

ἐπικείμενος is a more rarely used title.[2] Oeconomus, as was noted before, is restricted to ecclesiastical estates. Pronoetes was, like dioecetes, probably used with its etymological meaning in mind. The cognate noun, πρόνοια, is often used with reference to estate administration.[3] Finally there is the title hypodectes, collector, which states quite frankly the owner's chief interest in his property. It is the title of Count Ammonius' manager at Aphrodito; and in two documents, one from the Apion property, it occurs as a kind of further definition of pronoetes.[4]

Our most complete picture of the workings of an estate comes from the Apion poperty. The present chapter will, therefore, be mainly a description of the management of the Apion estate, citing such parallels from other estates as occur. The Apion estate was probably fairly typical, except that its large size probably demanded a more elaborate organization than the average estate would have. Unfortunately our general impression of the immensity of the Apion estate is not supported by strictly statistical evidence. We have some hint, however, of the extent and amount of the property involved. In formal documents the Apions use the phrase "landowner also at Oxyrhynchus" to distinguish themselves from those who were landowners at Oxyrhynchus only.[5] The estate extended through at least four nomes. The papyri from Oxyrhynchus relate to the administration of its affairs there and in the neighboring Cyno-

[1] P. Ox. 1134.

[2] P. Stud. Pal. xx, 209; P. Ox. 1892; P. Klein Form. 929.

[3] *E. g.*, P. Ox. 1900; 1985; 1987-1988.

[4] P. Cairo, 67138-67139; P. Ox. 136, 15; P. Klein Form. 529.

[5] *Cf.*, *e. g.*, P. Ox. 137 and 140.

polite nome.[1] Scattered references attest the fact that it included land at Heracleopolis [2] and in the Fayum. This last section of the estate was comparable in organization to its holdings around Oxyrhynchus, and probably also in size.[3] A few figures confirm the general effect. In one record of the Apion group the excess of receipts over expenditures reaches the sum of 178 pounds of gold,[4] over four times the supposedly generous salary of the augustal duke of Egypt.[5] Each of the Apion pronoetae was in charge of a fair-sized area, and there were at least twenty [6] of these officials, probably many more.

It is fairly clear that the Apions were in general absentee landlords. When the owner interfered directly in estate business the fact was noted in the accounts. "To the convent of Abba Apollo by written order of our master the consul" is a phrase that occurs in one of our documents.[7] When the master visited Oxyrhynchus it was decidedly an occasion. One account mentions the 16 artabae of grain required "for the service of our lord and master" and the 1132 artabae used by the baker who provided for "our master the consul and those who came with him." [8] The estate sent its owner wine, and perhaps other provisions, under the name of *cellarica.* At least once, probably in the time of Strategius I,

[1] For Cynopolis see P. Lond. 776; P. Ox. 1861; 1913, 46.

[2] P. Stud. Pal. xx, 129; P. Ox. 150.

[3] BGU 305; 368; P. Stud. Pal. xx, 209; P. Klein Form. 1072; 1115; P. Ox. 1921.

[4] P. Ox. 1918, RI.

[5] 40 pounds (2880 solidi); Edict xiii, 3.

[6] The number which appears in P. Ox. 2032.

[7] P. Ox. 1913, 8-9; *cf.* 1911, 147-151; PSI 953, 70-71, and the frequent orders of the lady in P. Bad. 95.

[8] P. Ox. 1913, 26-27, 59-60.

this went to Constantinople,[1] but in the seventh century the cellarer's annual trip only took him as far as Alexandria.[2] The celebration of the lord's birthday by distributions of wine seems to have been a common custom and was followed on the Apion estate.[3] On the other hand, the evils of absenteeism are reflected in such a complaint as "the servants of my master refuse to do the bidding of my good master."[4]

There seems to have been a central administration for the Oxyrhynchus and Cynopolis districts of the Apion estate at Oxyrhynchus. There was an estate house there, probably nominally a residence of the head of the Apion family and actually a center of the management of his estate and, to some extent, of the life of his employees. We have references to the bath[5] and the wine cellar[6] which it contained. There seems to have been an estate kitchen,[7] which would probably indicate that at least some of the staff did not live in separate households of their own. Some similar establishment has left us a kitchen account, perhaps of the Persian period. The provisions used in one day were nine measures of sour wine, one sheep, one young pig, three birds, four pigeons, twenty-nine eggs, and one camel.[8] It may be noted here that there seems usually to have been, even in minor districts, a definite building as a center of estate administration. The word προάστιον, which perhaps in its exact

[1] PSI 953, 72-73; *cellarica* for the first indiction,—537-8 A. D. is a probable date for this papyrus since that is the only first indiction when one of the Apions is known to have been at Constantinople.

[2] P. Ox. 1904.

[3] PSI 953, 80-81 (Apion) and PSI 957 from another estate.

[4] P. Ox. 130.

[5] P. Ox. 148; 1002; 2015.

[6] P. Ox. 2044; 2049.

[7] P. Ox. 1000-1001.

[8] BGU 377.

sense means suburban house, but is not always confined to that meaning, is found in this connection. The Apion estate had one, apparently near Oxyrhynchus.[1] The patrician Sophia owned one in the village of the Syrians somewhere in the Fayum.[2] We hear of baths in such buildings,[3] and of a large one with a kitchen in the court.[4]

It is possible that the Oxyrhynchus papyri give us at least the name of the general manager of the Oxyrhynchite and Cynopolite area of the Apion estate. Formal documents addressed to the head of the Apion family usually contain the words " through Menas, his servant, who is acting for him and assuming for his master, the said all-esteemed man, the conduct and responsibility," i.e., of the transaction,—or of estate administration.[5] Since the documents in which this formula or its equivalent occurs extend over about a century[6] the position was probably held by successive members of the family.[7] Our evidence is not sufficient to determine whether they were merely agents for making contracts or general managers. The latter possibility is perhaps supported by a letter in which a certain Menas writes to two counts urging them to collect the embolé from the people of Nigru.[8] In any case, the Menas family were connected only

[1] P. Ox. 915; PSI 955, 2, 17.

[2] P. Klein Form. 1092.

[3] PSI 955, 2, 17; P. Ox. 915.

[4] P. Basel 19 (E. Rabel and others, *Papyrusurkunden der öffentlichen Bibliothek der Universität zu Basel* in *Abhandlungen der Königlichen Gesellschaft der Wissenschaften zu Göttingen*, Phil.-Hist. Klasse, N. F. xvi, 3, Berlin, 1917); *cf.* P. Ox. 1003.

[5] *E. g.*, P. Ox. 134; the same words for conduct and responsibility (ἀγωγή and ἐνοχή) occur in P. Cairo 67151, 90-91.

[6] P. Ox. 1984 is from 523 (or 508?) A. D., P. Iand. 49 from 619.

[7] As suggested in P. Ox. 1829, note to line 24.

[8] P. Ox. 1841; another possible reference to Menas in PSI 238. Wine issued to Dorotheus, brother of Flavius Menas, in PSI 953, 70-71.

with the Oxyrhynchus and Cynopolis district. Other representatives are found in Apion documents from the Fayum.[1]

For the other estate officials who are now to concern us we have much better information. The Victor-George correspondence, a series of letters which passed between various important personages on the Apion estate,[2] tells us about its higher officials. The date of the correspondence is probably fixed by a group of receipts belonging to the same series and dated in 618.[3] The daily operations of minor employees are illustrated by a number of receipts, accounts, and other documents.

The general supervising officials whom we meet are the landlord's agent and the dioecetes. It is not impossible that there was only one landlord's agent in the Oxyrhynchus-Cynopolis area. The word does not occur in the plural in any of our documents, while we do hear of dioecetae.[4] On the other hand, in the Victor correspondence, which probably comes, as stated above, from a single year, three landlord's agents appear,—Victor,[5] Sarmates,[6] and George.[7] Unless we are to suppose a rapid succession in the office there were probably several agents.

In any case, the landlord's agent was superior to the dioecetes. When the Victor who figures in the correspondence is only an illustrious secretary he uses in his letters to the dioecetes George such expressions as "learning that your magnificence had arrived at Cynopolis I decided to write and sal-

[1] *E. g.*, BGU 305; 368, P. Stud. Pal. xx, 209.

[2] P. Ox. 158; 943; 1844—1861; 1936; 1937; 1940; notes on the two hands used, etc., in the introduction to P. Ox. 1844.

[3] P. Ox. 152-153; 1904; 2010-2011.

[4] P. Ox. 138, 23.

[5] P. Ox. 1844-1854; 1937.

[6] P. Ox. 1861.

[7] P. Ox. 1936. There is also an unnamed landlord's agent in 1859.

ute your honored feet . . . I make you many reverences and kiss your honored feet."[1] When he becomes a landlord's agent he gives George orders in all his letters to him, and can use such phrases as "please be good enough . . . to send him to me, since, as the Lord lives, if anything happens to him you will pay the price."[2] Elsewhere we hear of a dioecetes taking preliminary steps in settling a dispute, final action being left until the landlord's agent arrives.[3] The defensor of Cynopolis, writing to the dioecetes George, speaks of "our common master, the glorious illustris and landlord's agent."[4]

The Victor correspondence gives us at least a general impression of the functions of the landlord's agent. He was apparently in control of financial matters,—seeing that the taxes are sent to Alexandria,[5] exercising some control over the accounting,[6] giving orders for the transfer of payments,[7] etc. For the arbitration of disputes he was apparently the highest authority on the spot to be called in.[8] He was naturally a travelling official. Two of our documents illustrate his hardships in this connection. In one of these Nilus, addressing the landlord's agent Sarmates, expresses concern for his health on his journeys, and sends eighteen bundles of asparagus "for your blessed table."[9] The other document is a letter from Victor to the estate storekeeper:

[1] P. Ox. 1855.

[2] P. Ox. 1854.

[3] P. Ox. 1867.

[4] P. Ox. 1880.

[5] P. Ox. 1844.

[6] P. Ox. 1845; 1854.

[7] P. Ox. 1848. Payments due to a bishop are transferred at his request.

[8] P. Ox. 1853; 1867.

[9] P. Ox. 1861.

Will your true brotherliness be good enough to send me from time to time some asparagus, since the vegetables here are rotten and disgust me? Will your true brotherliness please be sure to do this?[1]

It is probable that the estate was divided into districts, each one headed by a dioecetes. Among the documents which suggest this is a list of arrears in taxes of which appear two dioecetae, Count John and Count Theon.[2] Elsewhere we find several places grouped together, in one case in the district of Count Papirius, in the other in the districts of Counts Diogenes and Phib.[3] Dioecetae seem to have had charge of such general estate matters as prisons[4] and boats,[5] and were probably the authority immediately above the local managers in the collection of dues. We find them responsible for seeing that arrears come in,[6] and the proper persons to apply to for assistance in collection.[7]

The oeconomi and dioecetae of the church of Alexandria may quite possibly have been similar to the landlord's agent and dioecetae of the Apion estate.[8] It is not surprising however, that no other estate about which we have information had such a double set of supervising officials. The Apions and the church of Alexandria may well have been the largest landowners in Egypt.

It was not infrequent, however, to divide scattered es-

[1] P. Ox. 1849. 1851 is a similar order for wine.

[2] P. Ox. 1908, 10-11.

[3] P. Ox. 1147; 2031. The title of count seems to be commonly given to the dioecetae.

[4] In P. Ox. 1835, and perhaps in 1854, a dioecetes is asked to release persons confined.

[5] P. Ox. 1846.

[6] P. Ox. 1147; 1908, 10-11.

[7] P. Ox. 1856.

[8] Leontius of Neapolis, *Life of St. John the Almoner*, 35.

tates into districts under collectors. The property of the church of Hermopolis was apparently divided into μερίδες.[1] Estates scattered over several nomes would have a natural geographical division. The heirs of Flavius Cyrus, from whom the poet Dioscorus rented land, were represented by "Victor, presbyter, and pronoetes of Antaeopolite business."[2] Similarly Flavius Alexander, general, employed a diocetes of Oxyrhynchite affairs.[3]

On the Apion estate such collection districts become numerous and important. We may obtain a summary view of their working and the position and functions of the pronoetae in charge of them from the contract which was concluded between the deacon Serenus and the heirs of Flavius Apion in 583 A.D.[4] Serenus agreed to be pronoetes or collector for the estate of Matreus, together with the property belonging to the Apions in and adjoining the villages of Episemus and Adaeus, for one year. He was to conduct his dealings with the coloni under him in accordance with the rent roll (ἀπαιτήσιμον) transmitted to him, so as to collect all that was due, paying over the money to the estate cashier, and the grain to the estate boatman. A complete account of receipts and expenditures was to be submitted and Serenus, or his surety, was to make up any deficiency which might occur. Finally Serenus agreed to pay the 12 solidi which was customarily given for the position of pronoetes, and expected to receive the same salary as his predecessor.

Our other documents confirm and to some extent supplement the information of this contract. The district which is described as given to Serenus seems to have been fairly typical. Each pronoetes had under his charge one or more

[1] P. Lond. 1060; 1072; 1782-1785.

[2] P. Cairo 67327, 6.

[3] P. Ox. 1899.

[4] P. Ox. 136.

κτήματα of the Apion family, to which would often be attached their scattered property in villages. We hear of a pronoetes of "Teruthis and Theagenes and Eutychias and other adjoining places," [1] and of another of "Margaritus, Ambious, Maiouma, and other adjoining places." [2] The κτήματα of Ktesis and Mattus and the village of Dositheus appear in one account of a pronoetes; [3] in another the pronoetes of Leonidus reports expenses on two other κτήματα as well.[4] Two fairly complete accounts mention payments to the churches of six and eight places respectively.[5] A similar grouping of property is suggested by a list in which receipts are arranged under the headings "of the κτῆμα of Papsau," "of the κτῆμα of Chenetorius," "of the κτῆμα of Samacion," and finally "in the village of Petne." [6] Elsewhere we find the receipts *of* Thaesis followed by those *in* various villages, none of them more than a third of the first item.[7] The Hermopolis estate was apparently similar in make-up to one of these Apion κτήματα. Among the places on it which the account mentions, one, at least, a place called Thalmoon, is similar to one of the Apion holdings or κτήματα; and houses in a village are also included in the property.[8] Whether the pronoetes who administered the Hermopolis estate was, like those on the Apion estate, one of many such officials we have no way of telling.

From the point of view of his employers a pronoetes was

[1] P. Ox. 2019.
[2] P. Ox. 999.
[3] P. Ox. 2027.
[4] P. Ox. 1910 R.
[5] P. Ox. 1911; 1912.
[6] P. Ox. 1912.
[7] P. Ox. 1910 V.
[8] P. Bad. 95.

probably primarily a collector. The Serenus contract, in fact, uses the word hypodectes as a synonym of pronoetes, and Count Ammonius' manager uses that title exclusively.[1] Says a sixth century letter:

Send the pronoetae to the country to collect, telling them to have many solidi ready for me for, as the Lord lives, if I do not find that they have been very vigorous in collecting, I will punish them well.[2]

Another, in which the writer is directing his correspondent where to ask for payments, begins: " Don't think that I am cashier of the estate of the late James. It is the pronoetae who collect." [3] Their collections were primarily rents, either from farm land or from house property belonging to the estate. They would also take in some money from the sale of grain.[4]

The conditions under which coloni held the lands on which they paid rents to the pronoetae are rather obscure and probably varied. Tenancy at will is attested by at least one document,[5] and frequently occurs in leases of the period. On the other hand, the actual holdings of *coloni adscripticii* were theoretically as permanent as their own status was. Custom, in any case, seems to have had considerable influence. Occasional difficulties naturally arose. One of our documents is, at least in part, a memorandum explaining why certain Apion fields which had been sown " from ancient and immemorial time " by the men of Pempo, a κτῆμα of the divine house, had now been transferred to other cultivators. The estate had demanded 1 solidus per aroura on

[1] P. Ox. 136, 15; P. Cairo 67139 vi R. etc.

[2] P. Ox. 1840.

[3] P. Ox. 1931.

[4] P. Ox. 1914, 6-7; P. Cairo 67139, ii R, iv V.

[5] P. Ox. 1941.

plough land and 3 solidi on vineyards.[1] Apparently some claimed that the obligation to furnish wine[2] sufficiently covered the extra value of vineyards. The rent which the men of Pempo had offered to pay was at the rate of 1 solidus per aroura on all their land.[3]

The pronoetes was allowed to make reductions in the amount demanded, whether wholly on his responsibility or subject to approval there is no way of determining. The estate was thus enabled to make allowances for agricultural accidents,—a failure of the inundation,[4] land injured by the collapse of the dikes,[5] vineyards overgrown with grass,[6] etc. On the other hand, the pronoetes sometimes made the peasant's lot harder by demanding extra payments, somewhat parallel to the perquisites, usually in kind, which are often added to the rent in sixth century leases.[7] Serenus was to collect 15 artabae on the hundred for the measure used in making collections.[8] The men of Pempo had found themselves saddled with extra charges on each solidus of rent of five-eights of a karat for the landlord and seven-eights for the pronoetes. And to make it worse figures were juggled by turning the rent for this purpose into the standard which would make it amount to the greatest possible number of solidi.[9]

But the pronoetes was much more than a mere collector.[10]

[1] P. Ox. 1915, 4-6, 21-23.

[2] For which see P. Ox. 1896 and p. 119, *infra*.

[3] P. Ox. 1915, 24-25.

[4] P. Ox. 1912, 175-176; P. Bad. 95, cols. 22-23.

[5] P. Ox. 1911, 193-205.

[6] P. Ox. 1911, 91; 1915, 7.

[7] *E. g.*, P. Lond. 1694-1695; 1698; 1770; P. Stud. Pal. xx, 218; PSI. 936.

[8] P. Ox. 136, 29-30. Gregory the Great attempted to suppress such charges on the papal estates (*Epistolae*, I, 44).

[9] P. Ox. 1915, 22-23.

[10] Gelzer's "Steuererheber" (*Studien*, p. 87) is shown by more recent documents to be much too narrow.

Alike under the Apions, under Count Ammonius, and under the owners of the Hermopolis estate, we find pronoetae making most of the estate disbursements in their districts. They pay salaries and wages, issue the estates' donations to the local churches, provide for the repair of machinery, the construction of cisterns, and building operations generally, purchase reeds for newly planted vines, and are sometimes used by the central management to pay for items on the general estate account.[1] It is probable that pronoetae managed many of the relations with peasants in which formal documents mentioned only the estate management. The pronoetes is not usually referred to in acknowledgements of loans, but in at least one case we have a receipt showing that it was he who actually paid out the money.[2] Receipts for the issuing of machinery are addressed to the proprietor personally, but in many cases such expenses appear in the accounts of pronoetae.[3] It seems probable that under favorable circumstances the pronoetes, representative of the estate in so many matters, had considerable influence in the life of the district. The letter in which Philoxenus, pronoetes of Pakerke, is instructed to bring about an arbitration is perhaps typical.[4]

Some information is available as to the salary and length of service of pronoetae. A few records of salary payments to Apion pronoetae remain. The money payments are somewhat under 2 solidi,[5] the grain allowances 24 artabae.[6] There must obviously have been other emoluments to make it profitable for Serenus to take a position for which he had to pay 12 solidi. Probably the perquisites which the men of

[1] P. Ox. 1910-1913; 2027; P. Bad. 95; P. Cairo 67138-67139; 67062.

[2] P. Ox. 206; *cf.* P. Amherst 149.

[3] *E. g.*, P. Bad. 95, *passim*; P. Cairo 67139 vR, 24; P. Ox. 1911, 160-164.

[4] P. Ox. 1839.

[5] P. Ox. 1912, 130; 2027, 25, 46.

[6] P. Ox. 1910, 7; 1912, 130.

Pempo objected to give us at least a hint of how he recovered. The application of the same rate which we find in that document to the total collections of one of our accounts of a pronoetes would produce an income of 30 solidi, twenty-one and nine-sixteenths karats;[1] and presumably there were other sources of a similar nature. If the Serenus contract is typical, Apion pronoetae were engaged for one year. If that was the case they were frequently reappointed. In an account covering three successive years, nine pronoetae are mentioned, one holding the same position for three years, and at least two of the others being in charge of the same district for two years.[2]

The districts of the pronoetae were rural. However, the rent collector for the city property (ἐνοικιολόγος) occupied a position fundamentally analogous. Although we do not possess any accounts of rent collectors we see them making payments to estate employees precisely as the pronoetae did.[3] The rent collectors were apparently given authority to conclude leases,[4] and such supplementary agreements as might be necessary. Such was the contract between Menas, rent collector of the estate of the most glorious general Theodosacius, and Cyricus, pork-butcher of Arsinoë, which provided that Cyricus was to be compensated for the money he had spent on his house if Menas turned him out, but not if he left voluntarily.[5] Rent was usually paid annually, sometimes semi-annually.[6] Estates, like the smaller landlords who

[1] In P. Ox. 1915, 22-23, ⅞ karat on the solidus; total in P. Ox. 1911, 207, 847 ½ solidi. The actual receipts in any year would be less because of remissions, classified in the accounts as expenditure.

[2] P. Ox. 1916.

[3] P. Ox. 1043; 1904.

[4] BGU 305 (Apion); P. Ox. 1038 (Flavia Euphemia).

[5] BGU 3.

[6] Cases of the latter method; P. Klein Form. 266; 763; 795; 802.

figure in the leases of this period, rented shops, workshops, or single rooms as well as whole houses.[1]

The finances of so large an organization as the Apion estate were naturally rather complicated. In managing them the estate had to depend largely on its own staff. One of the most remarkable differences between Byzantine and Roman Egypt is the disappearance of the bankers of the ealier period. In the three volumes of papyri from sixth century Aphrodito the word τραπεζίτης does not once occur; and Aphrodito, although in the Byzantine period only a village in legal status, was a place of some importance. To be sure, there were some remains of the older banking houses. Money lending was still carried on,[2] and it is barely possible that Oxyrhynchus still had a public banker.[3] For the normal business of collection, deposit, and disbursement, however, a great estate had to be its own bank.

The titles which we meet in this connection are those of chartularius and banker. Chartularius was perhaps rather a professional than an official term. We may distinguish in our documents three main groups of chartularii. The title is several times given to holders of other offices. We hear, for example, of a chartularius and landlord's agent,[4] and of a dioecetes and chartularius.[5] The most numerous references to chartularii, however, connect them with the central financial management and bookkeeping of the estate. In one of these cases the chartularius is also called cashier;[6] and it seems extremely probable that those who were called cashiers, as indicating their function, were also referred to

[1] PSI 81; P. Klein Form. 763; 875.

[2] *Cf.* the family founded by Eulogius, chapter iii *supra*.

[3] P. Ox. 2028.

[4] P. Ox. 156.

[5] P. Ox. 1847; 1853.

[6] P. Ox. 2010.

as chartularii, as indicating their qualifications.[1] Finally, in a third group of documents chartularii appear in a rather humble position. In two cases we hear of their supervising the vintage, in one of these clearly occupying a subordinate position under the landlord's agent.[2] Elsewhere a chartularius is collecting taxes under the authority of the dioecetes.[3] Probably the best reconciliation of these three uses of the title would be to suppose that the word chartularius properly designated a person's skill in keeping accounts, whatever position he might be holding at the moment.[4]

In view of their functions we should probably describe the τραπεζῖται as cashiers rather than as bankers, since they were presumably at the head of the central financial administration of the estate. We do not hear of more than one cashier at a time in the Apion documents, and it is not impossible that there was only one, at least for that part of the estate which was managed from Oxyrhynchus. The Apion cashiers known to us by name may be listed as follows:

| | |
|---|---|
| Philoxenus | 535 [5] A. D. |
| Anastasius | 552-557 [6] A. D. |
| John | 580 [7] A. D. |
| Macarius | 612 [8] A. D. |
| Menas | 618 A. D.[9] |

[1] In three exactly similar documents we have, P. Ox. 2010, a chartularius and cashier; P. Ox. 2011, a chartularius; P. Ox. 2045, a cashier.

[2] P. Ox. 1859; 2059.

[3] P. Ox. 1855.

[4] Or perhaps it indicated a man employed in the financial department of the estate. This is rather unlikely, however, since it would scarcely cover the case of the dioecetes and chartularius. In the next century chartularius was to come into official use as the title of the men who directed the accounting offices for upper and lower Egypt at the headquarters of the Arab government. (P. Lond. 1447, 137, etc.).

[5] P. Ox. 143; 205.

[6] P. Ox. 145; 1911, 212, 216; 1914, 7-8, 14; 1970.

[7] P. Ox. 144.

[8] P. Ox. 151; 2045; P. Amherst 157-158.

[9] P. Ox. 153.

Tentatively, at least, the accounting and banking of the Apion estate as carried on by its chartularii and cashiers may be considered together. With further information we might perhaps discover that there were two separate offices, the chartularii keeping accounts, the cashiers handling money; but the two activities related in any case to the same business operations. The first stage in Apion accounting was the "rent roll of the glorious house (ἀπαιτήσιμον τοῦ ἐνδόξου οἴκου)." It was apparently a permanent document,[1] but on the other hand was sent out by the chartularii to the pronoetae, perhaps because of the changing holders of that office.[2] It is quite possible that we have a fragment of this rent roll in a document which is apparently a list of amounts payable by the peasants of a κτῆμα. Fields, dove-cotes, a tannery, and an oil press are charged on individuals, while the rent of the palm trees and a charge "for the indictions," perhaps the taxes, are given as single items divided among the members of the community.[3]

The pronoetes then made his collections, did his business, and turned in the surplus to the estate cashiers. Apion pronoetae apparently turned in their money in irregular installments, presumably to avoid having too much on hand.[4] Our three preserved accounts seem to suggest a financial year ending in Phaophi.[5] The pronoetes at the end of the year's business wrote up his account. The account of receipts probably merely reproduced the rent roll, as we shall see shortly.[6] The expenditures could be arranged in several ways. They had probably originally been entered day by

[1] P. Ox. 1915, 3-4.

[2] P. Ox. 136, 17-18.

[3] P. Ox. 2037.

[4] Which might be dangerous; *cf.* P. Ox. 1853.

[5] P. Ox. 1911, 212-215; 1912, 162-164; 1914, 8-14.

[6] See p. 101, *infra*.

day,[1] and the year's account might simply summarize month by month.[2] Accounts of Apion pronoetae usually, however, show some attempt at classification. They begin with payments to the local churches, which one account puts under a heading " for sacred purposes," [3] and tend to group together salaries, remissions of rent, expenses of cultivation, purchases of machinery, and similar classes. The best preserved account follows the order just given,[4] but items often come in out of place, and even some Apion accounts show very little trace of any order at all.[5] The account from the Hermopolis estate is in general similar to one of the Apion accounts, except that, covering four years, it does not repeat the income in full each year, twice giving only the total. We have first the income for the eighth year of the indiction cycle, then the expenditures for the eighth and ninth. Tax payments are put first, and the other items roughly classified. The estate was then divided, at least for accounting purposes, and the rest of the document gives us first the receipts of the Προτάμου δωρεά for the tenth indiction, then its disbursements for the tenth and eleventh, and then the same items for the πρόσοδος τῆς μακαρίας.[6] It is charitable to assume that the records from the estate of Count Ammonius are only rough notes to be used in drawing up the final account, though at two points they include brief summaries of the grain receipts and expenditures.[7]

When his account was turned in the pronoetes had to wait

[1] P. Cairo 67141 and P. Stud. Pal. x, 251 are such day books.

[2] P. Ox. 2027.

[3] P. Ox. 1910, 2; 1911, 71-75; 1912, 115-119.

[4] P. Ox. 1911.

[5] *E. g.*, P. Ox. 1913.

[6] P. Bad. 95. The arrangement is summarized in Schnebel " Agricultural Ledger," p. 34 (but ια in 398 is an obvious mistake for ι).

[7] P. Cairo 67139 iv R, vi R.

until it was checked up. With the account he seems to have submitted the slips on which it was based, receipts and orders for payments. We hear of these under the names ἐντάγιον and πιττάκιον, which apparently covered any kind of small financial document.[1] Orders for payment may also be called ἐξοδιασμοί[2] or ἐπιστάλματα[3] or simply letters.[4] The pronoetes would have kept the orders for such items of expense as had been thus covered,[5]—the Hermopolis estate distinguishes others as ἄγραφα,—and probably had to show a complete set of receipts. Such a requirement would be the most natural explanation of a document in which a rent collector, having paid his own salary, gives himself a receipt for it.[6]

From one of the letters of the Apion landlord's agent Victor we gather that official support was useful at this accounting:

> See, I have sent the son of Abraham of Kl. . . . with his πιττάκια; and will your true brotherliness make up his account and let him go quickly without trouble and not allow the chartularii or anybody else to injure him?[7]

Safe past investigation, the honest or favored pronoetes received a statement. A specimen of this type of document has survived in which Justus of Oxyrhynchus assures the pronoetes Phocas that he has paid in full the fifth part of the revenue of Justus' late mother-in-law.[8]

The estate cashiers and chartularii were the normal dis-

[1] For examples, *cf.* PSI 284; P. Ox. 136, 22, 36; 1911, 216; 1988, 25; PSI 238; P. Cairo 67166, 19.

[2] P. Bad. 95, *passim*. (*cf.* Schnebel, "Agricultural Ledger," p. 36).

[3] BGU 675; PSI, 953, 70-71.

[4] P. Stud. Pal. xx, 125.

[5] P. Stud. Pal. xx, 125, "Keep this letter to remind you."

[6] P. Ox. 2008.

[7] P. Ox. 1845.

[8] P. Klein Form. 97; *cf.* P. Ox. 1134.

pensers of such money as was paid out from the central estate office. Donations,[1] salaries,[2] and payments for construction of dikes and cisterns[3] are recorded. They were responsible for sending the tax payments to Alexandria,[4] and presumably for sending on to the proprietor the year's profits. It is quite possible that we have a general account of the Oxyrhnychus district of the Apion estate in a list headed "receipts of pronoetae," the total receipts being 20,010 and 13/96 solidi.[5] Preserved with it is what may be a general account of the expenses of the central office, perhaps for another area or another year.[6]

The estate cashier made loans, probably for the estate's profit, if for anybody's. In one of our documents the cashier Anastasius issues 4 solidi to two mechanics of the Apion staff, to be repaid at their next pay day. The transaction is without interest, which would make it an advance rather than a loan.[7] Loans were also made to peasants. Thus in 582 A.D. Aurelius Ptollion, colonus of Ambious, borrowed 2 solidi from the heirs of Flavius Apion through his representatives, pledging all his property as security.[8] The way in which this accommodation might increase the estate's control over its coloni appears in the petition of Anoup, perhaps one of the most human documents in the whole series of Apion papyri, which relates to the comparatively large sum of 15 solidi borrowed by Anoup to replace his cattle which had died.[9]

[1] *E. g.*, P. Ox. 145.

[2] P. Ox. 152; 1904; 2045.

[3] P. Ox. 2035.

[4] P. Ox. 144; P. Amherst 157.

[5] P. Ox. 1918, V, I, 12.

[6] P. Ox. 2032; 1918 R.

[7] P. Ox. 1970.

[8] P. Iand. 48.

[9] P. Ox. 130.

It seems that the existence of even these estate cashiers enabled the officials of the estate to issue something comparable to a check. In 618 the estate agent Victor bought three horses at the village of Sephtha, giving in return an autograph πιττάκιον, on receipt of which the cashier Menas paid out the sum of 9 solidi.[1]

Certain principles of accounting and management may be noticed on the Apion estate, and some of them can be paralleled from other places. So far from any tendency to abandon the use of money, the Apion estate seems definitely to have preferred to have its income in cash rather than in kind. Two of our accounts of pronoetae show an administration so arranged as to leave a large surplus in money and a small surplus in grain, which is then promptly sold.[2] Numerous items for the purchase of grain occur elsewhere, in what is apparently a list of expenses, and perhaps indicate that sometimes there was no surplus in that department and grain had to be bought for sowing, etc.[3] Apparently the estate was satisfied with insufficient collections in kind in other departments also, since at least once it bought the wine which it then sent on to the proprietor.[4] A grain deficit appears once in one of the divisions of the Hermopolis estate.[5]

The accounts are managed in what seems to us a peculiar method, apparently with the aim of altering the credit side as little as possible from year to year. Both on Apion property and on the Hermopolis estate remissions of rent are listed as expenditures, the full theoretical amount standing

[1] P. Ox. 153. P. Cairo 67058, vi 20 and 67289 are possibly similar transactions, referring respectively to the village of Aphrodito and to an unnamed proprietor in the Thebaid.

[2] P. Ox. 1911, 209; 1914, 5-7.

[3] P. Ox. 2032.

[4] PSI 953, 72-73.

[5] P. Bad. 95, 491, 527.

under receipts. This is even continued where a remission has become permanent, and may be described as made "as usual".[1] The same group of standing remissions recur in this manner throughout the Hermopolis account.[2] Probably for the same purpose of avoiding changes the Apion estate seems to have kept separate accounts for properties which it had acquired from various owners. Thus, lands in various parts of the estate which had formerly belonged to a certain Diogenes were kept as a separate unit.[3] Probably this habit explains the curious fact that revenues which were collected by one pronoetes sometimes belonged to the district of another and were transferred to his account.[4]

A somewhat similar motive led to the custom of having expenses of the central administration assigned to be paid by pronoetae so that the money did not have to pass through the hands of the cashiers. The pronoetes of Apelle paid sums quite large in comparison with what he received himself for the salaries of the chartularii John and Jeremias;[5] and a third of the price of grass seed bought for the estate was paid through Julianus, pronoetes of Actouariou.[6] Parallels may probably be found in the orders which were issued by various proprietors, including the divine house, to pronoetae and rent collectors to pay salaries,[7] and in the receipts which we have for such payments.[8] It is probably an

[1] *E. g.*, P. Ox. 1911, 85, 87-88.

[2] Listed by Schnebel, "Agricultural Ledger," p. 39.

[3] P. Ox. 1910, 25-26; 1911, 53, 115; 2024, 6; 2055, 39. Diogenes is perhaps the count (and dioecetes?) of P. Ox. 2031, 1, perhaps the author of 1935. The account of Cephalas, to which various pronoetae contribute, was perhaps the same kind of thing (P. Ox. 1916).

[4] P. Ox. 1911, 209-210.

[5] P. Ox. 1911, 152, 155.

[6] P. Ox. 1913, 36-39.

[7] *E. g.*, P. Klein Form. 961; 1069; PSI, 196-197; 217.

[8] P. Ox. 1043; 1904; P. Klein Form. 87; 267.

estate in the Fayum which provides us with a list of the salaries of various personages,—three dioecetae, the chartularius, etc.,—giving under the names a list of villages from which, it would seem, they were to collect.[1] Sometimes the idea was even applied to individual tenants. A lease from the Fayum apparently included a messenger's salary as part of the rent.[2] Similarly a certain colonus John, somewhere in the Lycopolite nome, conducted a regular cashier's account with his landlord stating how much of his rent he had paid out on order and how much still remained.[3]

The principal items of income in kind on an estate demanded an administration roughly paralleling the administration of its money. The Serenus contract suggests that the boatmen held the same position in regard to grain that the cashiers did in regard to money. To some extent they seem to have provided a kind of estate grain bank, like the public thesauri of an earlier period, though the importance of this was reduced by the general use of money.[4] It was the boatman Menas who issued the grain which the Apion estate loaned to the village of Tacoma in 550 A.D.[5] Boatmen elsewhere make or order payments of grain for landlords.[6]

Wine on the Apion estate was apparently delivered directly by the cultivators at the estate cellars.[7] The wine of an estate was usually in charge of a butler (οἰνοχειριστής) or wine dealer (οἰνοπράτης). Part of the wine would be sold, both the Apion family and the imperial estates being in the retail wine

[1] P. Stud. Pal. x, 138.

[2] BGU 364.

[3] P. Cairo 67289.

[4] See *supra*, p. 100.

[5] P. Ox. 133.

[6] P. Ox. 1071; 1947-1948.

[7] P. Ox. 1896, 21.

business.[1] The rest would be kept for estate expenses, and paid out by the butler either in accordance with a standing schedule,[2] or by special order. We hear of wine being issued by the Apion butler Phoebammon in 590 A.D. to a group of bucellarii, to Alexander for nine days' work, and to groups of people, probably laborers, (164 in all) from different points on the estate.[3] Painters, stone-cutters, messengers, dioecetae, admirals, are among those who received wine on various estates.[4] The higher officials of the Apion estate were probably allowed to draw at will from the estate wine cellars.[5] The Apion butler kept strict accounts of receipts and expenditures, if the terms may be used in this connection. Among the accounts which have been preserved one records the disposition of 1843 .διπλᾶ of sour wine which were removed from his cellar. They came from the village of Adaeus and from six Apion κτήματα and were distributed among the three cellars of the gooseherd, the two cellars of the storehouse, the cellar by the gate of the estate house, and the cellar of the xenodocheion.[6] Another is apparently the central wine account, recording the issue of 36,622½ διπλᾶ (including 1343 of sour wine). The butler himself took in addition 73½, presumably at the rate of one measure on every five hundred, and the checker of wine jars was given five measures as part of his pay. The rest of the account then lists wine given out for pay and rations, in donations to churches and monasteries, by special order of the proprietor, etc. A column of money expenses perhaps refers to pro-

[1] P. Ox. 1973; 1131. *Cf.* P. Cairo 67168, which concerns wine sold by a monastery at Hermopolis to a Libyan bishop.

[2] Such as P. Ox. 2051.

[3] P. Ox. 150; 2012.

[4] PSI 193; P. Klein Form. 1129-1130; 1132; 1160.

[5] P. Ox. 1851.

[6] P. Ox. 2044.

ceeds of the sale of wine, kept on and paid out from the butler's account.[1]

Oil might be the subject of similar accounting in a large enough establishment. We have two series of orders for the issue of oil, one, described above as probably from a property of the church of Arsinoë, consisting of fifty-one slips addressed to "Cyriacus, deacon and oil dealer,"[2] the other, less extensive, probably from a private estate.[3] Oil was issued both as part of the pay of employees and for special expenses.[4] Estates that did not produce oil probably used it less freely for pay. The Hermopolis estate bought oil for the rations of its slaves,[5] and oil for lamps appears in accounts elsewhere.[6]

In addition to the men in charge of grain, wine, etc., the Apion estate possessed officials with the title μειζότερος whose functions are not entirely clear. They are probably to be distinguished from both the village officials and the general estate managers elsewhere who bear the same title. Perhaps they may best be thought of as men at a particular place in charge of such estate stores from the various departments as were there assembled for use. The estate agent Victor wrote to one of these personages for asparagus, and again for wine, and again to send something needed for a vineyard.[7] It was perhaps one of these μειζότεροι to whom the

[1] PSI 953.

[2] P. Klein Form. 898-945; 1074-1076; see *supra*, p. 46.

[3] BGU 960-968; P. Klein Form. 1100 and Ostraca 1603-1605 are similar documents.

[4] The Cyriacus series contains many items for pay of the sixth indiction, usually 6, 12, or 24 sextarii, and others for traveling and other special expenses.

[5] P. Bad. 95, 379, 503.

[6] P. Stud. Pal. x, 251.

[7] P. Ox. 1849; 1851; 1850.

butler Serenus issued fifty διπλᾶ of wine.[1] Another μειζότερος was instructed by Victor to order the headman of a village to take security for some brickmakers who had just run away leaving their work half done,[2] and finally a letter to the landlord's agent Sarmates reports:

They brought a horse for Crommydion to Cynopolis, and it is with Theodore the μειζότερος there, since it cannot yet be brought here.[3]

Since Crommydion was a place [4] we should perhaps conclude that Nilus, the author of this letter, who with it sends his correspondent some asparagus, was himself the μειζότερος representing the estate there.

The main outlines of the general management and banking of an estate must be filled in by a survey of the numerous employees which its various other activities required. An apparently professional group is that of the lawyers, who are several times mentioned in our documents. On the Apion estate the scholasticus Theodore of Cynopolis received, about the year 555, an annual present of 50 artabae of wheat, along with two others, Gerontius and Theodore, son of Gratianus, the latter of whom had the pleasant experience of having his retainer doubled.[5] In the year 612 we hear of boatmen making a trip to Alexandria to bring down a rhetor.[6] Yet it is certain that these lawyers were by no means always employed in that capacity. In at least one case we hear of two nomicarii as contractors of part of the estate stable,[7] and

[1] PSI 191.

[2] P. Ox. 158; *cf.* P. Ox. 943.

[3] P. Ox. 1861.

[4] P. Ox. 1921, 16.

[5] P. Ox. 1913; for Gerontius, *cf.* PSI 786. Scholastici on the Hermopolis estate, P. Bad. 95, 324.

[6] P. Ox. 151.

[7] P. Ox. 2024, 10-11.

elsewhere they appear in connection with the agricultural administration.[1] We cannot, however, draw a hard and fast line between lawyers and the notaries who drew up formal documents.[2] Probably, in any case, the large landowners had less occasion to employ lawyers, in the strict sense of the word, than we might suppose. Laws and courts seem to have been regarded by the country people of Byzantine Egypt with a not unjustified suspicion.[3]

An important body of the employees of a large estate was connected with the boats and horses which it used. In addition to shipments of produce for sale, and of goods and money for taxes or for the use of the proprietors, the business of a large estate would require considerable traveling on the part of the staff. In one short Apion account we hear of servants going with letters from Oxyrhynchus to Heracleopolis and the Fayum, and of a messenger being sent, apparently with bread, to the Thebaid.[4] Other business required regular trips at least to Alexandria.[5] The estate stable was apparently intended to provide for most of this traveling. In a contract dating from 610 to 611 a certain John agrees for one pound of gold to take care of the βαδιστικον στάβλον of Apion III, his chief duty being "to provide months for the distinguished diocetae and illustrious chartularii and the servants who go on any kind of estate business."[6] It is rather curious that the dioecetae are mentioned and not the landlord's agents. Perhaps we may infer from the document in which the estate banker pays for

[1] P. Ox. 2032, 9, 16, 25.

[2] *Cf.* P. Klein Form. 3; 347; and the practice of Dioscorus at Antinoë, as it appears in the Cairo papyri in documents from his office.

[3] *Cf.* P. Ox. 136, 38-39; Wenger, *op. cit.*

[4] P. Ox. 1921. Another trip to the Thebaid is mentioned in PSI 955, 26.

[5] PSI 953, 68-69; P. Amherst 157-158.

[6] P. Ox. 138.

horses bought by Victor that the landlord's agents were allowed to keep stables of their own, more or less at the estate's expense.[1] Apparently allowances in money or kind for traveling expenses were regularly given, presumably for food and lodging for horse and man. The *bucellarii* who went to Alexandria with the Apion tax payments took wine for thirty days with them.[2] A note from the patrician Sophia orders a letter-carrier who is going to Alexandria to be paid for fifteen days' expenses and the food of one horse.[3]

To what extent the Apion estate stable was run as a unit is not certain. It apparently consisted of at least two divisions, an ὀξὺς δρόμος and a βαδίστικον στάβλον.[4] The first is designated by the phrase which was the customary translation for *cursus velox,* the government express post for official purposes.[5] Probably on the Apion estate it was a service of especially good horses, for important letters, etc., and the other division of the stable provided the horses used for ordinary riding around the property. It seems probable that estate horses were kept at different points on the Apion estate. The estate evidently had stables at least at Crommydion and Cynopolis as well as at Oxyrhynchus.[6] A letter protesting that the estate has only one horse besides the three grooms' horses, which are only good for burden, is perhaps more intelligible if we suppose that it refers only to a part of the estate.[7] Grooms appear in various connections in our documents, but of details as to how they worked we have

1 P. Ox. 153.

2 PSI 953, 68-69.

3 P. Klein Form. 1096.

4 John in P. Ox. 138 takes charge of both. The patrician Sophia also uses the second phrase (P. Klein Form. 1095).

5 See discussion in Gelzer *Studien*, p. 88.

6 P. Ox. 1861.

7 P. Ox. 1858.

none, except a reference to payment of a veterinary,[1] and a letter in which we are told that Victor has sent a groom to recover a stolen horse.[2] It is barely possible that the Apion estate is the source of a document in which someone in charge of a stable reports on changes,—horses bought, sold, transferred, or dead.[3]

Something similar seems to have existed on other estates, although our information is small. We have a contract in which the stableman Serenus undertakes the management of the stable of Flavius Serenus of Oxyrhynchus. Unfortunately, no details are given of his duties. He was to receive 80 artabae of wheat for himself and the grooms for one year, 9 solidi for barley and vegetables, 80 jars of wine, and half a solidus for green fodder.[4] Two letters concerning the management of a stable perhaps indicate that it was customary for the grooms in a large establishment to be paid through the man in charge of the stable.[5] It must be left undecided whether we have humility or economy in a document in which a bishop's horse is apparently taken from the oil press of the church.[6]

Grooms are not unnaturally the letter-carriers we hear of most frequently,[7] though a guard is also mentioned in this connection.[8] Persons not important enough to have other employees at their disposal would have to send letters by anyone who was traveling in the right direction.[9]

[1] PSI 954, 14.

[2] P. Ox. 1854.

[3] P. Ox. 900.

[4] P. Ox. 140.

[5] P. Ox. 1862-1863.

[6] P. Klein Form. 963.

[7] P. Ox. 1861; 1921.

[8] P. Ox. 1858.

[9] *Cf.* BGU 1039, where the writer excuses himself for making a report before the facts were all in on the ground that the man who brought the letter left too soon.

The drivers of the other animals besides horses that we hear of were probably mainly employed for moving goods.[1] The Apion family owned camels, as we learn from an item for the pay of camel-drivers in the account of a pronoetes.[2] So also did the church of Arsinoë, and probably most other proprietors.[3] The oeconomus of that church contracted and paid in advance for its mule driving; [4] and a few other references to estate mule drivers and ass drivers have survived.[5]

The trip between Oxyrhynchus and Alexandria was apparently usually made by water,[6] although estate boats undoubtedly existed chiefly for the transportation of goods. The collection of grain has been mentioned before, and we hear of ecclesiastical estates in the Fayum sending their arax and beans off to market by water.[7] The estate of a certain Nonnous in the Fayum possessed a stolarch (admiral),[8] as far as I know the first occurrence of this title in private use since the stolarch of Apollonius the dioecetes seven hundred years before.[9] Boats are sometimes referred to by the captain's name,[10] sometimes by type. An Apion account contains payments to the sailors of the Carian boat and the large and small *liburni*.[11] Special kinds of boats

[1] On these animals *cf.* Schnebel, *Landwirtschaft*, pp. 332-339.

[2] P. Ox. 1911, 156.

[3] Church of Arsinoë, P. Klein Form. 907. Elsewhere P. Klein Form. 1079; 954; 304; P. Bad. 95, 70; P. Cairo 67141, I, V.

[4] P. Klein Form. 324.

[5] P. Klein Form. 954; P. Rainer 112.

[6] P. Ox. 144; 1846; 151.

[7] P. Klein Form. 1125; 1134.

[8] P. Klein Form. 1129.

[9] P. Cairo Zenon 59048. (C. C. Edgar, *Zenon Papyri* in *Catalogue général des antiquités égyptiennes du musée du Caire*, Cairo, 1925-1928, 3 vols.).

[10] *E. g.*, the boats of Damianus and Albil, P. Klein Form. 904; 908; 1074.

[11] P. Ox. 2032, 52-54, 75.

mentioned include a fishing boat[1] and "the boats of the canal," no doubt smaller than those used for river traffic.[2] We hear of a harbor in connection with the Apion estate, though the estate's relation to it is not clear.[3] It is possible, since we have few references to the pay of sailors, that estate owners in general followed what seems to be the policy of Flavius Theodore at Antaeopolis who leased his boat for no particular sum, the captain doing the owner's business, and presumably making his own living by other commissions. The boat, on which the captain intended to live, is described as "of 300 artabae burden, more or less, with a mast and yard, sail, various ropes, and a one-pronged [?] anchor, covered with mats of rushes."[4] The longest trips we actually hear of are those from Oxyrhnychus to Alexandria; but Flavius Theodore's boatmen agreed to go out of the country if necessary, though perhaps that only means out of the province of the Thebaid.

In a large establishment the higher officials would have subordinates, secretaries, messengers, etc., at their personal disposal. On the Apion estate the dioecetae had a secretarial staff,[5] and even the pronoetae have their subordinates. Their accounts include payments to foremen (ἐργοδιῶκται),[6] and at least sometimes they had bucellarii under their direction.[7] A letter addressed to a newly appointed pronoetes gives us a little view of their staff:

Let Phib stay with you to teach you the business until I learn

[1] P. Ox. 1846.
[2] P. Klein Form. 902.
[3] P. Ox. 1846.
[4] P. Lond. 1714.
[5] P. Ox. 1913, 64.
[6] P. Ox. 1911, 82-84; 1912, 130; PSI 954, 53.
[7] P. Ox. 1839.

what decision I should give him. Let the messenger of Justus stay with you until he has finished his year.[1]

Messengers (σύμμαχοι) were apparently fairly numerous. The patrician Athanasius employed seventy-eight, some of them perhaps in connection with his official position, probably that of Duke of the Thebaid;[2] and the Apion family had at least thirty-four.[3] There was a chief messenger (ἀρχισύμμαχος), although in one Apion document where he is mentioned he receives the same pay as his fellows, one-third of a solidus per month.[4] The "messengers of the chief messengers" whom we hear of were perhaps those who had not been assigned to special duty under any other estate officials.[5] Messengers appear in public as well as in private service;[6] and the title once occurs in the feminine.[7] The functions of messengers require no profound analysis. They are sent to see that a boat is repaired,[8] to help in making collections,[9] or to arrange for the transportation of men and property. This arrangement of transportation best explains the connection in which a group of messengers went with the Apion cellarer on his annual trip to Alexandria.[10]

The estate baths, bakeries, oil presses, etc., usually required attendants, although these estate services were sometimes rented out. The bathman whom we occasionally hear

[1] P. Ox. 1838.

[2] P. Ox. 1920.

[3] P. Ox. 2045.

[4] P. Ox. 2045. The title also occurs in P. Ox. 2051 and 1933; in P. Klein Form. 271 a presbyter is chief messenger of the church of Hermopolis.

[5] P. Ox. 1904.

[6] *E. g.*, messengers of villages, P. Klein Form, 90-92, etc.

[7] P. Klein Form. 395.

[8] P. Ox. 1846.

[9] P. Ox. 1856.

[10] P. Ox. 1866; 1871; 1904; 1931.

of was perhaps sometimes a personal servant.[1] Estate buildings might require doorkeepers;[2] and presumably it was heirs to estates who required nurses.[3]

Slaves do not seem to have been very common, although there were still some in great households. Curiously enough several of our references to them show them carrying on businesses of their own—a slave of Flavius Apion renting a house at Oxyrhynchus,[4] a slave of Cyril, tribune of Arsinoë, borrowing money from another member of the household,[5] or a slave of the patrician Athanasius in the Thebaid holding a government position.[6] The Hermopolis estate owned slaves who received food and clothes, but the purposes for which they were used are not stated.[7]

1 *E. g.*, P. Ox. 2006.

2 PSI 956, 37; P. Bad. 95, 174, 438, 479.

3 P. Klein Form. 1065; P. Bad. 95, 73, 441, 481.

4 PSI 709.

5 BGU 725.

6 P. Cairo 67166; and *cf.* BGU 669, referred to, *infra*, p. 113.

7 P. Bad. 95, 62, 74-75, 108, 468, 503-504.

# CHAPTER VI

## The Estates in the Social and Economic Life of Egypt

At many points the estate management which we have been looking at came in contact with the life of Egypt. These relations with the activities which would have gone on even if the estates had not existed are various and interesting. The estates took a hand in irrigation, in the growing of wheat, and the planting of vines. They employed or dealt with various trades,—potters, builders, brickmakers, carpenters, smiths, plumbers. In the oil-presses, mills, bakeries and baths which they operated they went into business themselves. Secondly, the estate owners had by their position considerable influence in the corporate life of village, nome, and province. Finally, there were contacts of various kinds between the estates and the church.

We may look first at the ways in which the Byzantine estates came in touch with Egyptian agriculture. They seem to have assumed the chief responsibility for the minor irrigation work which had to be carried on in their own property. Private dikes were erected from time to time;[1] but most of our information relates to cisterns and irrigating machines. The *lacus* is a common feature in descriptions of agricultural property in this period.[2] From

[1] P. Bad. 95, 332.

[2] *E. g.*, P. Cairo 67097 R, 2; 67107; 67170; P. Lond. 1003; BGU 669. The last document is an interesting though somewhat obscure petition from a decurion of Hermonthis, relating to machinery erected by a slave of the church which trespassed on a cistern on his property.

the lack of definite information in any one case we are left in some doubt as to what kind of construction we should imagine. Sometimes the lacus seems to serve a whole κτῆμα;[1] at other times we hear of the *lacus* of a field,[2] which is more in accordance with what we should imagine from earlier documents.[3] Possibly cases of the former class only mean that there happened to be only one such cistern in the κτῆμα in question.

A special professional group, the "rivermen" (ποταμῖται), were concerned with the construction of irrigation works.[4] There seem to have been enough of them at Arsinoë to form a guild,[5] and the estates probably hired them for particular jobs. If we may judge from one Apion account, the rivermen could be hired in groups.[6] At other times, indeed considerably more often in our documents, cisterns were erected rather as building operations.[7]

The provision and maintenance of irrigating machines is one of the most regularly recurring items of expense in estate accounts.[8] Both shadufs and sakiyehs appear to be mentioned. Who was responsible for the actual operation is less clear. In one case we hear of a special remission to the peasants outside the gate because they, "are to do the

[1] Note the *lacus* of various estates in P. Ox. 2035, *lacus* of Tarouthinus in P. Ox. 134, *lacus* of Aron in B. Bad. 95, 224.

[2] *Cf.* P. Ox. 1911, 96, 166-168, and the *lacus* of the orchard of Cenembatus, P. Bad. 95, 216.

[3] *Cf.* P. Ryl. 157 (A. S. Hunt, *Catalogue of the Greek Papyri in the John Rylands Library, Manchester* (Manchester, 1911-1915, 2 vols.) and Schnebel, *Landwirtschaft*, pp. 273-274.

[4] Schnebel, *Landwirtschaft*, pp. 64-65.

[5] BGU 295. For guilds in this period see Theodor Reil, *Beiträge zur Kenntnis des Gewerbes im hellenistischen Ägypten*, Leipzig, 1913, pp. 189-197.

[6] P. Lond. 1808; P. Bad. 95, 332; P. Ox. 1911, 157-159.

[7] See *infra*, pp. 123-125.

[8] P. Ox. 1911, 160-164, 169-174; 1913; P. Bad. 95, *passim*; P. Cairo 67139.

irrigation into the orchards and fields from their own property instead of [having it done by] the estate oxen of the glorious house ".[1] Elsewhere we have a receipt addressed to an official of the Apion estate in Heracleopolis for pay for irrigation carried out on land of one of the vine-dressers of the estate,[2] though this may refer to construction, *e. g.* of ditches. The receipts for new parts of machines addressed to the estate management of the Apion and various other Oxyrhynchite estates always speak of the machines as under the charge of the peasant who makes out the receipt, and presumably they were operated by him.[3]

For the major grain crops seed was sometimes advanced. Individuals[4] or villages[5] might be the recipients of this bounty. Count Ammonius' steward regularly set aside grain " for the season ".[6] Accounts of Apion pronoetae terminate with a note of the grain reserved out of this year's crop for next year's sowing. There does not seem, however, to have been a regular system of advancing seed to tenants such as had existed in connection with the royal peasants of an earlier period.[7] At least the great irregularity in the proportion of the amounts reserved to the total received would lead to this conclusion. In three accounts, for example, we have 300 artabae reserved out of 5054, 42 out of 1535½, and none

[1] P. Ox. 1913, 1-5.

[2] P. Klein Form. 86.

[3] P. Ox. 137; 192; 194; 202; 1899-1900; 1982-1991; P. Lond. 774-776, P. Iand. 50; PSI 60; 179.

[4] P. Ox. 1976; P. Klein Form. 52.

[5] P. Ox. 133; PSI 471.

[6] P. Cairo 67318 ii R, 34-36, iii R, 26ff; 67139 ii V 15-17 "grain of the count, ninth indiction, taken by Menas for the sowing of the season." The amounts are fairly constant,—in two years 141, and 149 artabae.

[7] For which see Schnebel, *Landwirtschaft*, pp. 120-121.

out of 1313¾.[1] Part of the seed grain would have been used for the estate cultivation shortly to be described. The advances recorded may be regarded, tentatively, as loans in case of need or as special favors. A case of the latter occurs on the Hermopolis estate, on which Aganthon of Cenembatus was annually charged 4½ karats for seed and granted a remission of the same amount.[2] Leases of the period frequently provide that the landlord is to furnish this seed,[3] but we can scarcely argue from them that the practice of large estates was the same.

Fruit and vegetable crops were raised. Palms are sometimes mentioned in estate accounts.[4] On the Apion estate they were apparently among the items which the peasants of a κτῆμα paid for jointly.[5] Orchards sometimes occur. Both in the Apion accounts and in the documents from the Hermopolis estate their irrigation is prominent.[6] There were vegetable gardens on the Apion property.[7] The κτῆμα in which one of them was located went by the suitable name of Vegetable Island.[8]

[1] P. Ox. 1910, R, 16-17; 1911, 218; 1914.

[2] P. Bad. 95, 41, 420, and 100, 205, 451, and 497.

[3] *E. g.*, BGU 308; 840.

[4] *E. g.*, P. Bad. 95, 38; P. Ox. 1911, 86; *cf.* Schnebel, *op. cit.*, pp. 294-300.

[5] *Cf.* P. Ox. 2037, apparently part of a rent roll, where the items for palms are in the form " for rent of palms and other [trees?], of 7-47/48 solidi," so much, usually ⅝ of a solidus (2, 6, 7, 15, 18, 20, 24, 29). The amounts preserved only reach 4-⅜ solidi, but the document is not quite complete and the crucial figure, perhaps amounting to several solidi, is missing in one case. 1911, 86.

[6] P. Ox. 1913, irrigation of the three orchards outside the gate in 6, 16-17, 22-23, 68; P. Bad. 95, irrigation of the orchards of Cenembatus and Thalmoon in 134, 138, 216. On orchards *cf.* BGU 255.

[7] P. Ox. 1913, 17, 68; 1917, 46 (rent paid in vegetables), 55, 116-117; P. Amherst 149.

[8] P. Amherst 149; island, of course, in the sense of specially fertile area. Vegetable Island is here said to be opposite Oxyrhynchus, and the

Direct cultivation carried out by employees of the estate is known; but it appears to have had no great place in the economy of our period. One list of expenses from an unknown estate refers to its "self-sown (ἰδιοσπεῖραι) arourae," in connection with which items for clearing off brushwood and for sowing appear.[1] The αὐτουργία of the Apion estate was probably estate cultivation, but we lack details. Under the title we hear of the purchase of grass seed for two Apion properties, presumably for the provision of fodder for the estate stable.[2] The word occurs as a heading in two accounts. In one we are only told of money issued in connection with certain fields on the κτήματα of Tarousebt and Lucius, about 45 arourae in all.[3] In the other, which is from an account perhaps covering the whole estate, the payments for αὐτουργία are merely recorded as made to various individuals and groups. They include both the fodder collectors, who are again, we may infer, in need of grass seed, and the people of various κτήματα[4]

Some estates managed their own flocks and herds. An unknown proprietor at Aphrodito has left an account into which are written several reports of shepherds,—number of sheep, how many male, how many female, how many born in the winter, and how much wool produced.[5] The church of Arsinoë seems to have employed a number of shepherds.[6] Chickens were kept, possibly only to feed important people.[7]

orchards and gardens in P. Ox. 1913 are just outside it,—perhaps producing for the city market.

[1] P. Stud. Pal. x, 251, b, 4-6.

[2] P. Ox. 1911, 178-180; 1913, 36-39. For the verb αὐτουργεῖν *cf.* P. Flor. 282.

[3] P. Ox. 1911, 107-137.

[4] P. Ox. 2032, 68-88. The total, 191 solidi, is repeated in P. Ox. 1918, 26.

[5] P. Cairo 67141.

[6] P. Klein Form. 910; 911; 928; 937; Oxhert in 934.

[7] P. Ox. 1913, 26-27; *cf.* P. Bad. 95, 173.

Dovecotes were constructed[1] and then usually rented.[2] Their main use was to provide fertilizer for the peasants.[3]

The production of grapes and wine was of considerable importance throughout the history of Greco-Roman Egypt.[4] On the Apion estate wine was produced on a large scale. We hear of vineyards in the village of Adaeus,[5] on the κτήματα of Cotuleeius,[6] Chenetorius,[7] Leon,[8] Tarousebt,[9] Vesobthis,[10] Papsau,[11] Samacion,[12] the Woolcarders,[13] Ostracinus,[14] Parthenias,[15] Teruthis, Thaeagenes, and Eutychias,[16] Neon, Pera, Leonidus and Limenias,[17] Skytalitis, Crarium, Little Parorium, Psempekle, and Great Mouchis,[18] and probably of one just outside Oxyrhynchus.[19] The vineyards were evidently scattered, as we might expect, among other kinds of land. One account indicates that in the property to which

[1] BGU 962.

[2] PSI 954, 5; P. Ox. 1911, 65; 1912, 70; 2037, 21; P. Bad. 95, 33-34, 204, 413.

[3] Schnebel, *op. cit.*, pp. 85-86, 342.

[4] *Ibid.*, pp. 239-241.

[5] P. Ox. 2044.

[6] P. Ox. 1911, 91, 104, 182, 184, 187.

[7] P. Ox. 1912, 57.

[8] P. Ox. 1896; 2044.

[9] P. Ox. 1911, 182, 191.

[10] P. Ox. 1912, 127.

[11] P. Ox. 1912, 29, 127; 1982.

[12] P. Ox. 1912, 85, 88.

[13] P. Ox. 1913, 29-32, 51-53.

[14] P. Ox. 1917, 80.

[15] P. Ox. 1990; 2044.

[16] P. Ox. 2019, 19.

[17] P. Ox. 2044.

[18] PSI 954, 7, 22, 40-42.

[19] P. Ox. 1913, 33-35.

it refers there were 61½ arourae of ploughland and 4 of vineyard.[1] Irrigating machines are frequently described as "supplying water to vineyards and arable land."[2]

The actual cultivation was mainly in the hands of coloni, with whom the estate frequently dealt in groups, the vine-dressers, or the peasants and vine-dressers, or the κοινόν of the vine-dressers of such and such a place appearing in accounts.[3] This does not, of course, mean that peasants mentioned only by name were not also cultivators of vines. Although leases of vineyards in this period call for payments in wine only,[4] dues in grain and money were exacted from vine-dressers as from other coloni. Their special obligation, however, presumably their principal one, was the provision of the estate flow (ῥύσις) of wine. One of our documents is an acknowledgment of this responsibility, eight coloni of Leon addressing Flavius Apion and agreeing

> by this our written deed of security to be ready, on our joint responsibility, to give to your magnificence to the account of the estate flow of the estate vineyards of our κτῆμα in the vintage of Mesore of the present tenth indiction, for the flow of wine of the (D. V.) eleventh indiction, 3000 eight-sextarius estate jars of wine, including the arrears of the present tenth indiction . . . and to deliver these in full at the cellar. . . . If we fail to do this we agree to pay for each Cnidian measure [amount missing] on the security of our property.[5]

Only at two points did the estate come in contact with the actual process of growing grapes and making wine. Ac-

[1] P. Ox. 1915, 4, 14.

[2] *E. g.* P. Ox. 1899; 1900; 1982; 1990.

[3] P. Ox. 2019, 19; 1912, 29; 2038, 20.

[4] Schnebel, "Agricultural Ledger," in *Journal of Egyptian Archaeology,* vol. xiv, 1928, p. 42.

[5] P. Ox. 1896.

counts from Apion property and from the Hermopolis estate and a letter to Count Ammonius' manager all refer to the provision by the estate of the reeds on which vines were commonly trained.[1] This issuing of reeds seems, however, to have been rather a special encouragement for the planting of new vineyards than a regular provision. In the two cases in the Apion accounts the reeds are definitely stated to have been issued for newly planted vineyards,[2] and at Hermopolis there is evidence that there was a large extension of the vineyards of the estate during the period to which our document relates.[3] Reeds used for this purpose seem to have required replacement about once in four years;[4] but this was presumably left to the peasants themselves. The Apion estate bought its reeds, as far as we know. The managers of the Hermopolis property, however, also encouraged the growing of reeds by their tenants.[5] An account from another estate at Hermopolis, otherwise unknown, lists thirteen reed-beds, which produced, however, less than half of the seventy-two bundles of reeds which it used, forty-six bundles being brought.[6]

With the work between planting and vintage the estates

[1] For which custom see Schnebel, *Landwirtschaft*, pp. 254-262. Reference to the purchase of reeds for Count Ammonius, P. Cairo 67062, 10; 67139 vR, 11.

[2] P. Ox. 1911, 175-177; 1912, 152-154.

[3] Note in P. Bad 95 the increase in the number of jars required from hundreds in the 8th indiction (115-116) to thousands thereafter (*e. g.* 235-236). Newly planted vineyards are mentioned at Aron (57, 161), Cenembatus (215), and Thalmoon (332) the places for which reeds are issued (Aron, 234, 315, Cenembatus 58, Thalmoon, 312, 233).

[4] Schnebel, *op. cit.*, p. 257.

[5] P. Bad. 95 records payments or remission of dues for newly planted reeds, 60, 165, 176, specifically at Thalmoon 163, 281, 347, and on the land of Sarapion of Cenembatus 203, 439, 450, 480, 496.

[6] P. Stud. Pal. xx, 147.

had no direct connection. Nor did they always assume responsibility at the vintage except to see that they got their share. Chartularii were often sent to supervise the vintage. A list of memoranda from an unknown estate includes the sending of a chartularius for the vineyard business.[1] In one of the Apion letters the chartularius Menas urges an estate agent

> if possible to order Pambechius and his partners from Seruphis to be spared [2] today and tomorrow until they finish their estate flow of wine, since they began today to gather their grapes and are producing a great flow of wine,

and the sooner they have finished, the sooner Menas can return.[3] τρυγητικά are sometimes heard of as extra allowances at the vintage for employees busy at that time.[4] Contrarywise, some Apion coloni seem to have been subject to special dues at the same period.[5] Once only, on an unknown estate, do we hear of the work of the vintage carried out by paid estate employees.[6]

The provision of jars by the estate is parallel to the frequent provision in contracts for the sale of wine that the purchaser is to provide jars, an obvious method of insuring that he gets the desired amount.[7] The numbers recorded give some idea of the quantities involved. The men of Leon, as we have seen, were to fill 3000 eight-sextarius

[1] P. Ox. 2059.

[2] What they are to be spared from is not clear; perhaps estate work elsewhere.

[3] P. Ox. 1859.

[4] PSI 953, 19; 956, 24-25; BGU 310; *cf.* P. Strassburg 40 for such vintage dues in a salary.

[5] PSI 954, 7, 12.

[6] BGU 1039.

[7] *E. g.* P. Lond. 390; 1001; P. Strassburg 1; P. Cairo 67104 is exceptional.

jars;[1] other Apion documents mention similarly large figures.[2] On the Hermopolis estate 2879 jars were issued for Thalmoon and 1954 for another property in the ninth indiction. Two years later the insufficient Nile of that year or some other reason brought the number required at Thalmoon down to 1852, although other vineyards now called for 2491.[3] The amount which an otherwise unknown oeconomus of St. Thecla's (church, hospital or monastery) paid for pottery, namely, 6 artabae and 8 solidi, should at the price we find elsewhere correspond to well over a thousand, perhaps well over two thousand jars.[4] A document from Aphrodito gives us some basis of comparison for the amounts. One hundred and twenty-six jars of wine per aroura occur in it as the rent of a vineyard.[5]

The contacts of estates with trades were numerous. We may group the trades concerned by the connections in which the estates required their assistance. The most important of these were its building operations, its supply of pottery, and the construction and repair of its agricultural machinery. For building the estates drew on the three crafts of house-builder (*οἰκοδόμος*), brick-maker (*πλινθευτής*), and carpenter (*τέκτων*), professions which inevitably overlapped. We hear of a *τέκτων οἰκοδόμος*,[6] and in a papyrus from the Fayum the patrician Sophia orders certain builders to be paid for the bricks which they have provided.[7]

All the estate accounts which have been preserved at any length show entries of payments to brick-makers and build-

[1] P. Ox. 1896.

[2] P. Ox. 1911, 181-192; 1913, 29-35, 51-53; PSI 1474.

[3] P. Bad. 95, 235-236, 370.

[4] P. Klein Form. 104.

[5] P. Cairo 67104.

[6] P. Klein Form. 176.

[7] P. Klein Form. 1092.

ers,[1] for whom apparently every estate of any size would have some work every year. With a single exception[2] there is no indication that the estate assumed any responsibility for the houses of its tenants. The estate structure most frequently mentioned, and apparently the most firmly built, on account of its connection with irrigation, was the *lacus* (cistern). "Send at once the builders with the men of Gessias to the estate, to complete the cistern and prevent the water from flooding the land," we read in a sixth-century letter from Oxyrhynchus.[3] In one place in the accounts of Count Ammonius the pay of a builder is followed by an item for the transportation of bricks for the cistern of the estate of Peto.[4] On the Apion estate we find these *lacus* of still more solid construction, large stones being bought for them in two cases.[5] The town houses of estate owners are represented in our documents by a bill headed: "Summary of expenses . . . of the cellars of the glorious house of our master the god-protected patrician, checked by Paul, priest of the holy church of St. Thecla, and carpenter, and Cosmas, προάστιον." [6] For a ἀρχιτέκτων in a village in the Fayum the patrician Sophia bought several boat loads of bricks of the best quality.[7] On another estate the dovecote

1 Apion, P. Ox. 1910, 5; 1911, 79; 1912, 122; 1913, 45, 63; Count Ammonius, P. Cairo 67138 iiR, 26; 67139 vR, 20, 25; Hermopolis, P. Bad. 95, *passim*.

2 P. Bad. 95, line 223, "to the builder of the ἔπαυλις of Alite, peasant, 5 karats."

3 P. Ox. 1834.

4 P. Cairo 67138, ii R, 26, 28.

5 P. Ox. 134; 1911, 166-168.

6 P. Stud. Pal. x, 259. The unexpected verb δοκιμασθεῖσι in the bill probably means that Paul and Cosmas were doing the work for cost plus so much, and wished to emphasize that they had gone over the account carefully.

7 P. Klein Form. 1092.

of Heracleon enlisted the labors of Sambas the carpenter and a group of sawyers.[1] Unfortunately, however, many of the records preserved speak only of payments to workmen without stating what job they were engaged on.

Stone is occasionally mentioned, for cisterns on the Apion estate,[2] elsewhere for a προάστιον.[3] For ordinary work bricks were used, either baked or sun-dried. The better type is specifically mentioned for one of Count Ammonius' cisterns[4] and in a few other cases, two of which at least are buildings of some importance.[5] The average barn or office was probably run up very simply.

Such evidence as we have seems to show that these building trade workers were generally independent craftsmen rather than estate employees. The two documents which refer to the obtaining of stones by the Apion estate for its cisterns suggest that stone-cutting in that part of Egypt was in the hands of guilds of stone-cutters. One is a contract in which John, κεφαλή of the stone-cutters, agrees to provide two hundred large stones for a solidus. The other is a reference to twenty karats paid "for the price of one hundred and fifty large stones bought from the stone-cutters of Trigeus."[6] Trigeus was itself perhaps part of the Apion estate, at least in its sphere of influence, and probably adjoined the Apion κτῆμα of South Trigeus,[7] while John was a native of the Apion property, although not stated to have been one of their coloni.[8] There is no indication, however,

[1] BGU 962.

[2] P. Ox. 134; 1911, 166-168.

[3] PSI 193.

[4] P. Cairo 67139, V R20.

[5] P. Stud. Pal. x, 259; P. Klein Form. 1092; P. Bad. 95, 460.

[6] P. Ox. 134; 1911, 166-168.

[7] P. Ox. 1911, 73, 85-87, 160-161.

[8] As formal documents usually seem to mention the fact if a man is a colonus, the argument from silence is here stronger than usual.

in either case that the stone-cutting transaction was not a free and open purchase.

It was apparently a matter of convenience whether one bought bricks or hired a brick-maker. The Hermopolis estate shows both procedures.[1] In the Fayum the Apion estate bought bricks.[2] At Oxyrhynchus its brick-makers and builders may have worked for it regularly; but apparently they did not work for it exclusively. In one of our documents the dioecetes Victor writes that two brick-makers have left their job and he orders that surety be taken so that they may not again leave their work half done.[3] Apparently they were engaged by the job and would move on to another job elsewhere when the work was finished. Reil's decision that the estates assembled a number of workmen instead of employing guilds perhaps needs some modification, although his point that the mere occurrence of plurals, " brick-makers and builders," etc., does not prove such employment is well taken.[4] The stone-cutters seem to have acted in a body; and we now have a receipt from three men on behalf of a group of brick-makers and builders acknowledging pay for several years from a pronoetes, probably of the Apion estate.[5] On the Hermopolis estate, on the other hand, when a cistern was constructed the pay of the builder, the wages of the laborers, and another item of expense were met separately by the management, which apparently proceeded on a different principle.[6] Only in one document have we a clear

[1] P. Bad. 95, 123, 126, 214, 216 and 460. In 323 we should probably read πλινθ (ουργοῖς), not πλινθ (οῖς) as the recipients of money.

[2] P. Stud. Pal. xx, 209.

[3] P. Ox. 158.

[4] Theodor Reil, *Beiträge zur Kenntnis des Gewerbes im hellenistischen Ägypten*, Leipzig, 1913, p. 91, note 8, and 175-176.

[5] P. Ox. 2007.

[6] P. Bad. 95, 224-228.

reference to builders permanently employed. This is an order for payment from the property of the church of Arsinoë which reads "issued to the four laborers, builders of Nilopolis, as pay for the sixth indiction twenty four xestae of oil."[1] These men, who are spoken of as ἐργάται as well as builders, may well be, like the ἐργάτης and πλινθουλκός of an earlier document,[2] semi-skilled workmen who could handle any minor jobs that came along. The whole system was apparently quite fluid. Every village probably had its builders,[3] and the estate managers were apparently able to find workers as they needed them.

The estates needed jars in large quantities once a year, at the vintage. We are not surprised to find that they bought their supplies from local potters. In one Apion document Sourous of Harpocras and the potters of Taruthinus provide jars for the vintage of Cotuleeius and Tarusebt,[4] in another Anoup of Toe furnishes those needed for the ἐποίκιον of the Wool-carders, Abraham of Great Parorius those for the vine-dressers of the vineyard of the προάστιον.[5] Pitch at times issued,[6] in addition to payment in money and grain. The patrician Strategius, almost certainly one of the Apion family, bought his wine jars from a potter of Arsinoë.[7] Similar items occur in the records of the Hermopolis estate,[8] and on two aparently ecclesiastical properties.[9]

[1] P. Klein Form. 930. [2] BGU 894.

[3] P. Ox. 2058 mentions four among the hundred-odd householders of Spania.

[4] P. Ox. 1911, 181-192; *cf.* P. Ox. 1912, 127-128.

[5] P. Ox. 1913, 29-35, 51-53.

[6] References in the last two notes; and *cf.* Reil, *op. cit.*, p. 40.

[7] BGU 368.

[8] P. Bad. 95, 115-116, 235-236, 313-314, 326, 370, 374.

[9] P. Klein Form. 104; 927.

The repair of irrigating machinery was probably a more regular item. Sweeps and waterwheels alike seem to have needed spare parts fairly often. Sometimes estates attended directly to the repair of their machines. Thus we find the Apion estate constructing or repairing the machine of the orchard of Pkemroch and a group of six machines outside the gate of Oxyrhynchus. A smith, a potter, and a carpenter were employed for the job.[1] Count Ammonius' manager bought iron for the equipment of his ὄργανα,[2] and the proprietors of the Hermopolis estate were always buying, sometimes apparently even renting, bits of machinery.[3] But at least at Oxyrhynchus estate machines were put under the care of a peasant and spare parts issued to him. Something approaching a standard form was in use for acknowledging receipt of implements by these peasants.[4]

With the help of this form we can watch the process. It is always expressed quite dramatically. The peasant realizes the need of a new axle, or whatever it may be, and goes up to the city. The proprietor shows a proper regard for the condition of his estate and orders the machinery to be issued, and now everything will be all right. Sometimes the actual issue is merely said to have been made by the person doing business.[5] In other documents the person is named and we see that we have a minor estate employee, the carpenter Phoebammon,[6] the monk Luke (on church property),[7] or

[1] P. Ox. 1913, 19-23.

[2] P. Cairo 67139 vR, 24.

[3] P. Bad. 95, 132-139, 219, 225, 336-338, 385-391, 464-466, 502. P. Bas. Copt. 1 illustrates the renting of machines.

[4] *Cf.* P. Ox. 1899 (Flavius Alexander); 1900 (Church of Oxyrhynchus); 137, etc. (Apion).

[5] P. Ox. 1982; 1985.

[6] P. Ox. 1899.

[7] P. Ox. 1900.

the mechanic Zacharias.[1] Two μηχανουργοὶ of the glorious house appear in one of the Apion documents as borrowing four solidi from the estate cashier, to be returned at their next pay day.[2] Their time was doubtless devoted to this part of the work of the estate. But in another group of these documents we are told instead that the axle required was bought "in the fields" and the price entered in the records.[3] Of the large number of pieces of machinery the purchase of which is recorded in the accounts of the Hermopolis estate only two are said to have been bought in Hermopolis.[4] We may probably infer local manufacture for the others. The evidence is not sufficient to indicate definitely the reason why estate employees did some of this work and not the rest. Except in one case the spare parts bought in the country in the Apion documents are axles, which were presumably easier to make. On the other hand, most of the purchases in the country are later than most of the cases at issue at Oxyrhynchus.[5] This would perhaps indicate a development or a change of policy.

A group of lesser trades are occasionally represented in our documents. A lead-worker was called in by the Apion family in 572 for various odd jobs, and we have his receipts for repairing pots and pans and pipes.[6] Work on boats is recorded only in the case of the completion of a skiff and the caulking and repairing of other boats which happen to figure in the accounts of the church of Arsinoe.[7] The Apion

[1] P. Ox. 1987.

[2] P. Ox. 1970.

[3] P. Ox. 1988-1991; P. Iand. 50; *cf.* P. Ox. 1911, 160-164, 169-174.

[4] P. Bad. 95, 132; these were bought for a new vineyard.

[5] Documents mentioning persons at Oxyrhynchus are dated in the years 497, 535, 543, 552, 587; those mentioning purchase in the country come from the years 557, 587, 590, 591, 616.

[6] P. Ox. 915; 1000-1003.

[7] P. Klein Form. 900; 901; 902; 904; 908; 920; 924.

estate bought mats and ropes from the monks of Abba Andrew's, an interesting contact with the industry which monks carried on mainly for their own discipline.[1] A fuller on the Hermopolis estate,[2] another employed by Flavius Serenus at Oxyrhynchus,[3] and a group of weavers working on the clothes of the Lord Serapion in an account of some unknown establishment [4] are our only representatives of the textile industry.

We may summarize by saying that for all skilled work independent craftsmen were usually engaged by the job. Probably fairly typical of the whole matter is the situation evident in the Arsinoë series, where various employees, shepherds, ox-herds, etc., are paid 12 or 24 measures of oil as part of their wages for the year, while the shipbuilders, caulkers, and bronze-workers receive smaller amounts for definite pieces of work.[5]

Another group of contacts occurs in what may be called estate services. Some of these had almost the character of commercial speculations; as for example the estate baths. Both public (municipal) and private baths existed in the sixth century. The city of Antaeopolis mentions in a petition, by way of illustrating its sad condition, that since it has been ravaged by the Blemmyes it has not had a public bath, and even the poorest have had to pay for the use of a private one.[6] In the Apion accounts the "estate bath of the great house" is known to us from its purchase of mats

[1] P. Ox. 148; 2015. On monastic industry *cf.* Leipoldt, *Schenute*, pp. 125-126, 136, 174.

[2] P. Bad. 95, 172; but note purchase of clothes in 468, 504.

[3] P. Iand. 43.

[4] P. Stud. Pal. x, 251, 9-10.

[5] P. Klein Form. 898-945; 1074-1076.

[6] P. Cairo 67009, v, 22-24; for the public bath of Alexandria, see Edict xiii, 15-16; for that of Oxyrhynchus, P. Ox. 1889, 8; 2040.

and ropes and the repair of its pipes.[1] This particular establishment may have been for the use of the family and estate officials. Almost certainly, however, the other baths we hear of were commercial propositions. Such was the bath in the προάστιον,[2] and those of the villages of Tacona and Ophis.[3] Sixty mirrors were bought for the bath at Tacona and eighty for that at Ophis in 621 A. D. Sometimes these estate baths were leased instead of being run directly by the estate. A letter addressed to the chartularius George illustrates the kind of situation which this might lead to:

Will your true brotherliness please see that the most illustrious Menas and Serenus, the most illustrious cashier, and Menas the procurator come to arbitration about the bath, and do not let the supervisor leave them until the one of them who owes the rent of the bath agrees with the glorious house to pay it? For Serenus, the most illustrious cashier, through the persuasion of his wife drove the most reverend Çollouthus out of the bath and having done what he was persuaded to do, will not go away. And as the Lord lives I do not leave the three, for they are paying the rent of the bath until the landlord's agent. . . .[4]

It is not surprising to find that large proprietors were more able to own oil presses than their tenants. The manufacture of oil was a seasonal occupation, requiring a plant which could only be used for one or two months of the year.[5] While, to be sure, it was at least not the universal custom for estates to make all their own oil,[6] ἐλαιουργοί occur

[1] P. Ox. 148; 2015; 1002.

[2] P. Ox. 915.

[3] P. Ox. 1921.

[4] P. Ox. 943.

[5] Reil, *Gewerbe*, pp. 140-144.

[6] Note, *e. g.*, purchase of oil in P. Bad. 95, 379, 503, etc.

as estate employees, issuing oil on the order of the managers.[1] But probably more important was the existence of oil presses maintained indeed by the estate, but rented to its coloni. There was an oil press at Thalmoon on the Hermopolis estate, from which rent was collected and for which machinery was issued.[2] In the Apion accounts there are two references to the rent of oil presses,[3] and a record of the provision of pounding stones for the estate oil press of Great Parorium.[4]

Quite similar was the relation of the estate to its mills and bakeries. These were the same, since millers and bakers formed one profession in Greek Egypt, as we may illustrate from an Apion document in which objects provided for a mill are stated to be for the bread making of the following year.[5] Sometimes, to be sure, we hear of baking done for a household by its own members[6] or by a baker hired by the day,[7] or given a larger or smaller amount of estate grain to turn into bread, and presumably paid in proportion.[8] But the large estate had its mills and bakeries. The Apion family apparently had a mill at Oxyrhynchus,[9] and owned such establishments in various places, sometimes rented to the people of a village, sometimes provided for the use of

[1] BGU 960-968; Wilcken, *Ostraca*, 1603-1605; P. Klein Form. 898-945, 1074-1076.

[2] P. Bad. 95, 23, 130, 220, 70.

[3] P. Ox. 1917, 100; "rent of the oil press of Pselemachis"; 2037, 31 "Sourous, ἐλαιουργός, for rent of oil press."

[4] P. Ox. 1913, 65-66.

[5] P. Ox. 1983. On the profession in general see Reil, *op. cit.*, pp. 150-158.

[6] *Cf.* Reil, *op. cit.*, pp. 154-155; P. Klein Form. 982; P. Cairo 67141, iv, 10.

[7] P. Cairo 67141, ii V, 8.

[8] P. Ox. 1913, 59-60 (*cf.* 2032, 77); perhaps P. Cairo 67139, iii R, 18, 28ff, P. Bad. 95, 167, 177.

[9] P. Ox. 1983, 17-18.

its own coloni.[1] The bakery of Thalmoon, like its oil press, belonged to the owners of the Hermopolis estate.[2] In a few cases we hear of a bakery both owned and operated by an estate. A document from the Fayum is headed "account of expenses of the bakery situated in the ἐποίκιον of Psineuris, belonging to our master the all-esteemed patrician, by John and Elias, bakers"; [3] and an Apion account refers to the payment of the workmen of the bakery.[4]

We have been occupied so far in this chapter in investigating the relation of the estates of Byzantine Egypt to various types of economic activity. We may now look at their more general relation to the life of Egyptian village and province. It is not hard from the Apion documents to construct the way in which estate property was scattered over the countryside. It presents itself to us very clearly in the description of the districts in charge of pronoetae in which we uniformly see a group of κτήματα or ἐποίκια and, connected with them, property in villages.[5] We may look at the former group first. In contracts and bonds relating to coloni we find that in every case they are stated to be from κτήματα of the estate, which are often also referred to as ἐποικια, never from villages.[6] In non-technical use ἐποίκια are smaller settlements, perhaps sometimes only farms. The ἐποίκιον is usually described as near a village,[7] sometimes as in its territory.[8] Sometimes it is of sufficient importance to

[1] P. Ox. 1912, 102; 1983, 10-12 "the estate mill under me and the other coloni of the estate."

[2] P. Bad. 95, 24, 97, 196, 202, 303, 309.

[3] P. Stud. Pal. x, 114.

[4] PSI 956, 39.

[5] See pp. 88-89, *supra*.

[6] List p. 75, note 4, *supra*.

[7] *E. g.* Psekes near Aphrodito, P. Cairo 67112.

[8] P. Lond. 1767.

have a secretary of its own.[1] But it is evident that a technical use had grown up at Oxyrhynchus in which three things went together; what was called, as a place where people lived, an ἐποίκιον, was, as a piece of property, a κτῆμα, and its inhabitants were *coloni adscripticii*. The combination is found in non-Apion as well as in Apion documents.[2]

It is a matter of definition whether we speak of these κτήματα as manors. They were the places, in any case, where the system which the previous chapters have described was applied in its full force. And the peasant who paid his taxes to Flavius Apion's pronoetes, watered his land with an estate irrigating machine, got his bread from an estate bakery and his oil from an estate oil press, and knew that the estate prison was waiting for him if he attempted to leave, this peasant was quite well aware what the system was. One or two further facts may be added about these properties. The serfs were headed by one or more φροντισταί, at least on each Apion κτῆμα, who to some extent supplied the lack of the village government which still existed elsewhere. We have unfortunately little information as to their position. They were sometimes paid by the estate,[3] but more frequently stood in the same relation to it as other coloni.[4] The fact, however, that a φροντιστής is mentioned first when a number of coloni are parties to a contract,[5] and that even the brother of such a personage spreads his position as such on the record,[6] is enough to show that they were in some way the first among the serfs of their hamlets. To some extent the Apion κτήματα

[1] BGU 846.

[2] P. Ox. 1896; 1911, 193; 1917, 83-84; 1983; 1985; 2019, 5; 2024, 7; 2029, 5, 10; 2037, 28.

[3] P. Ox. 2024, 7.

[4] P. Ox. 1911, 196; 1917, 83-84; 1935; 1985; 2019, 5-8; 2029, 5; 2037, 28.

[5] P. Ox. 1896.

[6] P. Ox. 1983.

seem to have adjoined villages, to which they had probably once belonged. At least Little Tholthis must have been near the village of Tholthis,[1] while the very name of Aetius' Little Teruthis[2] probably commemorates some fourth or fifth century landowner who gathered into his patronage a settlement perhaps formerly part of the village of Teruthis.[3]

We are at once reminded of the situation in 415 A. D. as the edict recognizing patronage describes it. The estates and the independent villages, *vici publici* or *metrocomiae*,[4] are apparently still here. But the prohibition against the purchase of land in villages by outsiders, though renewed in 468 A. D.,[5] continued a dead letter. It is probable that, officially and legally, the great landowners were in the villages merely proprietors on the same footing with everybody else; but the way was open for all kinds of influence. The loan of grain by the Apion estate to the protocometae of Tacona was without interest, but probably the estate saw somehow that its generosity was not unrewarded.[6] We have a letter to Dioscorus the poet in which some official of the village of Aphrodito apologizes for putting his name on a list from which his patron, a count, had ordered it removed.[7] The two cases of village notables thrown into estate prisons are sufficient to indicate what would sometimes be done.[8]

The Hermopolis estate seems to have had much the same make-up as the Apion property. Thalmoon was probably,

[1] P. Ox. 1985; village officials of Tholthis in P. Ox. 1831; 1948.

[2] P. Ox. 1983.

[3] P. Ox. 2025, 8, etc.

[4] See *supra*, p. 24.

[5] C. J. xi, 54 (1).

[6] P. Ox. 133.

[7] P. Cairo 67200.

[8] P. Ox. 1835; 2056.

although no descriptive term is used, similar to one of the Apion κτήματα. The estate owned not only land, but houses, an oil press, and a bakery; and it subsidized the church.[1] The rest of its property was perhaps more scattered and included houses in a village. We should probably not be wrong in imagining all over Egypt a similar dovetailing and mixture.

The importance of the great landowners is further illustrated in their relation to the nomes in which their estates lay. A few of our documents bear on the relation of the Apion estate to the city of Oxyrhynchus. An item in an account of 621 A. D. combines a member of the *curia* of Oxyrhynchus and the estate:

> To . . . formerly of the glorious house and of the most magnificent decurions, for a pair of muslins bought and given to the praetorium on account of the Persians in the 9th indiction, of six karats, the share of the glorious house, 1⅝ karats.[2]

It is perhaps too much to conclude from this that when a fund was raised from all Oxyrhynchus the proper contribution of the Apion estate was about a quarter. We are on firm ground, however, with some other pieces of evidence. A deputy defensor of Oxyrhynchus appears in one of our documents as a humble tenant of Apion property.[4] Elsewhere Menas, defensor of Cynopolis, in a letter to the Apion dioecetes, George, refers to a landlord's agent as "our common master." Menas seems to have received some kind of allowance from the estate.[5] As was mentioned in the chapter on the history of the family, several of the Apions

[1] P. Bad. 95.

[2] P. Ox. 1921.

[3] P. Ox. 1921.

[4] P. Ox. 1987.

[5] P. Ox. 1860.

were pagarchs and tribunes of the nomes where they owned property. When Strategius I held the position of pagarch during his official career at Constantinople he presumably exercised his local functions by deputy. We may perhaps assume that the μειζότερος Theodore, who holds the title some eighty years later, similarly represented his absent master.[1] The Apion family's interest in the hippodrome at Oxyrhynchus was probably both a natural consequence of their position in the city and a means of maintaining it. The circus factions seem to have played considerable part in Byzantine politics in Egypt as at Constantinople.[2] Unless the Apions changed their support from side to side, they subsidized both parties. In 552 A. D. one of their cashiers paid for an embrocation for the horses of the Greens and for other expenses.[3] In 618 A. D. they paid the starters of the Blues and at an earlier date (perhaps 538) provided wine for the grooms of that party.[4] There was an estate box in the hippodrome at Oxyrhynchus, guarded by a door-keeper.[5]

Somewhat more sombre is the picture which we get of the relation between the nome of Antaeopolis and its nobles. The fact, however, that the local poet Dioscorus of Aphrodito produced with equal facility poetic eulogies on officials and petitions against their enormities suggests that we ought to use with care documents of the latter class. About 550

[1] P. Ox. 1858; for exercise of the functions of pagarch by deputy *cf. infra*, p. 137.

[2] Rouillard, *op. cit.*, p. 191; John of Nikiou, *Chronicle*, 107-109. In 609-610 A. D. the Greens supported Heraclius, the Blues Phocas. When Nicetas finally conquered Egypt for the former, he followed up his victory by establishing peace between the factions. *Cf.* Maspero, *Histoire*, p. 43.

[3] P. Ox. 145.

[4] P. Ox. 152; PSI 953, 42.

[5] PSI 953, 62.

A. D. there were two pagarchs at Antaeopolis, Julianus and, to our great surpise, Patricia, who exercised her functions through her dioecetes Menas, who also received the title of pagarch.[1] Julianus is known to us elsewhere as an estate owner.[2] While the appearance of a woman pagarch does not quite demand the hypothesis that she inherited the position, she probably held it as an adjunct to her estate. Her possession of a private dioecetes shows that she was a landowner. The first round of petitions from Aphrodito deals with the attempt of Julianus to have that important autopract village under his financial control.[3] Towards the end of the decade 560-570 A. D. Menas was sole pagarch of Antaeopolis. Menas, it should be noted, was also an official of the provincial administration and his son, at least, styled himself landowner.[4] The rights of Aphrodito were again attacked. Dioscorus was ousted from his lands in the neighboring village of Phthla and obliged to leave the district.[5] A group of men from Aphrodito had gone to sell their cattle as usual in the market of Thinis. They were seized by the dioecetae of the illustrious Serenus and held in various prisons, finally in that of Antaeopolis, for large sums of money. In their petition addressed to the duke they appeal for corroboration of their statements to Apphous, notary of the duke's dioecetes Licinianus, who was with them in jail. It should be noted that Serenus is given no official title, and was almost certainly acting merely as a powerful landowner.[6] The same mixture of private and

[1] P. Lond. 1660.

[2] P. Cairo 67060.

[3] P. Cairo 67019; 67283; 67024.

[4] P. Cairo 67002 i, 6; P. Lond. 1714; accepting the basic chronology of these events as fixed in Maspero, "Les papyrus Beaugé," pp. 137-143.

[5] P. Cairo 67002 ii, with which *cf.* P. Lond. 1677; 1682.

[6] As is held by Gelzer, *Studien*, p. 92.

public activities continues in the next act. Menas breaks the dam on which the agriculture of Aphrodito depends and then attacks and plunders the town with "a force of robbers and civilians and soldiers (ληστρικὴ καὶ παγανικὴ καὶ στρατιωτικὴ βοήθεια)."[1] Perhaps not the least significant part of the struggles of Aphrodito was that some time before 548 A. D. it had supplemented its appeal to law by placing itself under the patronage of the empress. In order to fight the attacks of the local land-owning and office-holding aristocracy it attempted to have the imperial family on its side, not only in the public interest, but also in their own private interest as landowners.[2]

Provincial as well as local offices were often in the hands of the estate-owning class. There is evidence for a fair proportion of native Egyptians even among the augustals at Alexandria,[3] and wherever we have evidence the dukes of the Thebaid after 538 A. D. seem to have been Egyptian estate owners, as in the case of Apion in 550 or Athanasius some twenty years later.[4] Petitions and eulogies at least indicate the kind of phrases which might suitably be used of a noble and governing family. Says a petition to the duke of the Thebaid:

Your ancestors, full of mercy to those in need, were the treasure of the whole province, nourishers of the poor, merciful in their gifts to the needy, so that their unfortunate children should not die of famine.[5]

The poems of Dioscorus contain a few significant phrases, as when he exclaims "the general is not a foreigner,"[6] or

[1] Narrative of these events in P. Cairo 67002.

[2] P. Cairo 67283 (and introduction); 67002, ii, 14-15.

[3] Gelzer, *Studien*, p. 34.

[4] P. Lond. 1709.

[5] P. Cairo 67020, 10-11.

[6] P. Cairo 67097 V, 95.

hails the family of the pagarch Collouthus as rulers for a long time and tells us that they were known throughout the bounds of the Nile.[1]

The relations of estate owners and the church demand separate treatment. Some points are not clear; but others throw considerable light on the place of the estates in the life of the country. There is a good deal of pious phraseology, even in business documents. References to the coming year are made with a pious σὺν θεῷ, the equivalent of *deo volente*.[2] Apion landlords' agents regularly use the same formula with their title, thus ascribing to the proper source their exalted position,[3] and in several places other estate officials are given the same distinction.[4] The sign of the cross at the beginning of documents became an increasingly elaborate formula,[5] nor was it unnatural in Byzantine Egypt for a report on the inundation to begin: "I again bring your excellency the good news that the blessed fertilizing river of Egypt has risen by the power of Christ."[6] Unfortunately the scarcity of purely personal letters prevents our going far below the surface. We know that employees of the Apion family received the equivalent of Christmas presents;[7] but, except for one point which will be mentioned shortly, we can sketch their relations with the church but not their relations with religion.

[1] P. Cairo 67120 V, B. For further examples see Jean Maspero "Un dernier poéte grec d'Égypte: Dioscore, fils, d'Apollos" in *Revue des Études Grecques*, vol. xxiv, 1911, pp. 426-481.

[2] P. Ox. 133; 136; 137; 138; and documents of the period *passim*.

[3] P. Ox. 1845-1855.

[4] P. Ox. 1857 (μειζότερος); 1838 (pronoetes); 138 (contractor of the stable).

[5] P. Ox. 138; P. Grenfell II, 100. For the longer formula introduced under Maurice, see John of Nikiou, *Chronicle*, 99.

[6] P. Ox. 1830.

[7] P. Ox. 1857.

Men in orders were among those who lived on the estates as tenants or employees. When a whole community was absorbed into an estate the clergy of the place would be absorbed with it, especially since, in smaller places in Egypt of this period, the clergy were still farmers as well as priests.[1] A priest and a deacon are definitely stated in two of our documents to be Apion coloni,[2] and several others appear as tenants in estate records.[3] In the village where the Apion estate had interests it came in contact with the local clergy, either among the village notables with whom the estate dealt officially,[4] or as renters of its property.[5] Deacons appear several times as notaries,[6] and one as a pronoetes on the Apion estate.[7] The functions of deacons in administering the business of the church probably made such transitions into secular business easier for them than for the other clergy, although we do find a presbyter as collector in a city.[8]

The direct relations of landowners to ecclesiastical bodies and corporations are not wholly clear. Numerous donations to churches and monasteries appear in our documents. Every account of expenses of an Apion pronoetes opens with a statement of grain, sometimes of grain and money, issued to the churches of the district which he had in charge.[9] Wine was also given to some churches, though we cannot

[1] *Cf.* P. Lond. 1765 where a priest and a sub-deacon rent land as *γεωργοί*.

[2] P. Ox. 996; P. Lond. 778.

[3] PSI 180; P. Ox. 1911, 202; 1912, 22; 1917, 78; 2019, 13, 65.

[4] P. Ox. 2056; 1917, 5-6.

[5] P. Ox. 1917, 12, 19, 23, 26, 29. Probably most of the clergy at Ibion, the village covered in this part of the account, appear here as tenants.

[6] P. Ox. 134; 1961; 1985.

[7] P. Ox. 136.

[8] P. Klein Form. 960.

[9] P. Ox. 1910, 2-4; 1911, 71-75; 1912, 114-119; 2024, 5-7.

say whether this was universal or not.[1] These local donations are relatively small, the most considerable being one of 64 artabae to the xenodocheion of Leonidus.[2] A parallel is the grant of 6 artabae which the Hermopolis estate made annually to the church of Thalmoon.[3] These offerings seem to have been made, in general, to the churches of places which the estate owned rather than to those of villages where it merely held property. This may perhaps suggest that the donations were in lieu of ecclesiastical dues normally paid to the village church. This suggestion is supported by two receipts addressed to officials of unidentified estates, one to a landlord's agent for wine issued " for the first fruits of the same holy church," [4] the other to a pronoetes for wheat, barley and vegetable seed constituting " the prequisites of St. John." [5] In an Apion document the pronoetes of Nesus Leucadiou distinguishes, in the statement of what he gave to its church, between the 18 artabae which were paid for the great estate and the 6 artabae for the Diogenes property.[6] This would at least fit in well with the view that these payments were a charge on the land rather than a donation by the landowner. Some kind of payment to the bishop was due from Apion property. We learn this from a letter in which an estate official directed a subordinate to carry out the bishop's order that his *annonae* were to be given to a man who had many children and not enough to maintain them.[7] And sometimes land came to the Apion family already burdened with certain obligations, such as

[1] PSI 953, 8, 10, 11.
[2] P. Ox. 1910, 4.
[3] P. Bad. 95, 71, 175, 283, 349.
[4] BGU 693.
[5] P Klein Form. 80.
[6] P. Ox. 2024.
[7] P. Ox. 1848.

the gifts to the chapel of St. Serenus at Tarouthinus, which were made as directed by two sons of the bishop.[1] On the Hermopolis estate the 6 artabae which were given annually to the church of Thalmoon are a standing item, in contrast to the other donations, such as those to the doorkeeper of the new church, to St. Mary's, etc., which vary from year to year.[2]

Probably to be distinguished from these payments is another class of donations, usually considerably larger and usually directed to monasteries or institutions rather than to parish churches. A typical record in the Apion accounts is the following:

To the monastery of Abba Andrew as usual, instead of 50 solidi less 5 karats granted to them by written order of our master the consul, for the fifth indiction, year 233 and 202 [eras of Oxyrhynchus; 557 A. D.], 1000 artabae of wheat, and on the day of the great man 18 artabae[3]. . . .

Also to the monastery of Abba Andrew, by order of our master the lord patrician Strategius, from [produce of the fifth] indiction and for the present year as usual 100 artabae of wheat . . .

For the transportation of the 1118 artabae of wheat given to the monastery of Abba Andrew 1-½ solidi less 5-¼ karats.[3]

Two years before this, for some reason or other, the estate had been less generous, and this same monastery had had to pay an estate stableman for moving hay and chaff from the Apion barn to the monastery stable.[4] Wine was also given

[1] P. Ox. 1911, 92-95.

[2] P. Bad. 95, 71, 175, 283, 349. Other donations in 63 (perhaps a benefaction to a hospital), 69, 169.

[3] P. Ox. 1911, 147-151, 154. "The day of the great man" might have been the birthday of the head of the family, or perhaps the anniversary of the death of one of his predecessors.

[4] P. Ox. 146.

to monasteries;[1] and the hospital of 'Abba Elias received, apparently annually, 371 artabae of wheat.[2]

These documents raise the question as to the purpose of these donations. It is at least possible that some of them were intended to pay for requiems for deceased members of the family. The word προσφορά, which is the term most frequently used when these pious donations are given a definite name, had come to have a technical meaning in this connection, indicating either the eucharist or other requiem office or an endowment for the continuance of such.[3] An interesting will of the period shows us the chief physician of Antinoë directing that his heirs should pay the taxes on the aroura of vineyard which he left to a monastery to continue the services for the repose of his soul. This would presumably enable them to watch over the other provision that the monastery was not to use the income for other purposes.[4] Careful business men like the Apions might have preferred to keep the matter in their own hands and make their payments from year to year rather than run the risk inevitably involved in a perpetual endowment. Such was perhaps the arrangement adopted by Gerontius, a lawyer employed by the Apion family, whose heirs gave an annual προσφορά to the monks of Berku.[5]

We may consider it almost certain that the Apions and

[1] PSI 953, 9, 12, and perhaps 30-31, 82.

[2] P. Ox. 1898.

[3] Discussion in P. Ox. 1898, note to line 23, Preisigke *s. v.* But it should be noted that the use of προσφορά for the eucharistic offering is rather old in Christian literature. Moreover the phraseology in wills for examples see P. Ox. 1901, 50; P. Lond. 77, 57; P. Cairo 67003, 21; 67009; 67151, 124; 67312, 76; 67324, 4 is clearly ecclesiastical. Hence the use in this connection should be explained from its liturgical sense primarily, rather than from its legal meaning of "legacy."

[4] P. Cairo 67151, 101-160.

[5] PSI 786.

other great landowners made payments for this purpose, whether our documents happen to record them or not. The Byzantine Egyptians, however, were quite capable of distinguishing between mortuary funds and other pious purposes,[1] and it is quite impossible to interpret all the references as endowments for requiems. This is especially the case when pious donations are made to individuals, as to a blind man on the Apion estate.[2] Such cases are presumably to be classed with the other individual benefactions which we find recorded, gifts to widows and other persons in need, sometimes described under the heading of εὐσέβεια.[3] Motives were probably often mixed, as in contributions for public purposes at all periods. Rather charming is the wording of an inscription which records the beneficence of a member of the aristocracy in the Fayum:

> The good work of the paving of the holy church of St. Menas was completed under Abba Peter, Bishop, on Mesore 16, at the beginning of the 15th indiction. Lord, help thy servant Menas, general, and his children. Amen.[4]

There is some evidence to indicate that landowners acquired a certain amount of control over the ecclesiastical bodies which they favored with their patronage. Laymen, too distinguished to be employees, act as managers of church property. Count Ammonius is dioecetes of the monastery of Apa Agenius at Apollonopolis Parva, and acts through Apollos, his collector at Aphrodito.[5] Apollos himself

[1] As is done *e. g.* in P. Cairo 67312, 70-76.

[2] P. Ox. 1921, 5; for πολυβλέπων as meaning blind see Bell and Crum, "Greek-Coptic Glossary," line 269, and the passage from Chrysostom cited in the note.

[3] PSI 953, 61, 63.

[4] Rec. chret. 831 (Gustave Lefebvre, "Égypte chrétienne, iv Inscriptiens coptes et grecques" in *Annales du service des antiquités de l'Égypte*, vol. xi, 1911, pp. 238-250; p. 245).

[5] PSI 933; donation to this monastery in P. Cairo 67139, iv R.

founded a monastery and left the position of phrontistes and curator to his son Dioscorus;[1] and at Hermopolis we hear of a duke, Senouthius, as phrontistes of the church.[2] On the Apion estate we find, whether it is significant or not, that the oeconomus of the hospital of Abba Elias who signed the receipt for their donation to it was himself a notary of the estate. Elsewhere we find the estate able, under what circumstances is not quite clear, to use the archimandrite of a monastery as its agent in issuing bread to the people of Tarouthinus.[3] Most convincing is a letter from a hospital official, probably the oeconomus, in which the titles used indicate that either the Apion estate or some similar organization was in question. We are told that the people of the ἐποίκιον of Piahoth had come to the hospital and asked for a donkey, barley, and fodder. The writer points out that hospital revenue is for charitable purposes, not for donations to prosperous ἐποίκια; but they should of course have what they wanted "if they were assigned it by my lord and brother, the magnificent secretary, or by our common lord, the most glorious *illustris*."[4]

The picture presented to us shows the estates in touch with all sides of Egyptian life. They help or regulate the agricultural operations of their tenants. They are employers of skilled labor, owners of business enterprises, factors in the country's government, patrons of the church. But almost never, as far as we can tell, do they tend to be in any sense economically self-sufficient units.[5]

[1] P. Cairo 67096.

[2] P. Klein Form. 271 B.

[3] P. Ox. 1952.

[4] P. Amherst 154.

[5] The word *Oikenwirtschaft*, used for such "house economy" in the Rodbertus-Meyer controversy of a generation ago, was applied to these estates by Reil, *Gewerbe*, p. 23, and Wilcken, *Grundzüge*, p. 83; but its appropriateness is doubtful.

# CHAPTER VII

## Epilogue

We have seen how large a part the great estates played in Byzantine Egypt. What happened to them when that period came to an end? With the Mohammedan conquest Egypt returned to a more effectively centralized bureaucratic government than it had had since the days of the early Ptolemies. In such a system there was no longer any place for estates of the kind we have been describing. Even a glance at the Aphrodito papyri of the early eighth century[1] is enough to bring out the contrast. In the Byzantine papyri from the same place,[2] Aphrodito and Antaeopolis live their own turbulent lives with the distant duke of the Thebaid and the scarcely more distant emperor as occasional sources of regulation and interference. A hundred and fifty years later the pagarch of Aphrodito is scarcely more than an agent, directed at every step by orders from the caliph's governor at Fustat.

There is, to be sure, some evidence that there still existed among the Copts a class of land owners at least better off than their fellows. We still hear of Egyptians owning whole ἐποίκια.[3] The document from which we learn this is one in which the writer asks a person of importance, perhaps a bishop, to use his influence in favor of the writer's brother Germanus, who had been ordered by the emir to deliver a

[1] P. Lond. vol. iv.

[2] P. Cairo vols. i-iii.

[3] P. Lond. 1081.

certain number of horses from his estate. A similar taxation of landowners appears in a letter from the governor in which Basil, pagarch of Aphrodito, is ordered to impress carpenters and caulkers for the navy from " the city itself and the contributory villages and the notables " of his pagarchy.[1] The notables (ἐμφανοί) apparently constituted a definite class, since another order from the governor directed Basil to have a fine assessed by an ἐπίσκοπος and four ἐμφανοί.[2] It seems not impossible, moreover, that these Coptic notables may to some extent have continued to be an office-holding as well as a land-owning class. At least this same pagarch Basil was on occasion represented by his " landlord's agent and personal representative," Apa Cosma (patigeuches auō peprosopon),[3] although the former title may have lost its original meaning. But these survivals into the next period of Egyptian history are little more than curiosities. In general, the estates of the sixth century were one of the many features of Byzantine Egypt which passed out of existence when the soldiers of Amr came in.

The whole period of Byzantine Egypt derives a certain additional interest from the fact that it presents a kind of frozen development. If we attempt to pass judgment on the period at all we must regard it as an interesting beginning which never had a middle or an end. It would not be hard to paint a rather dark picture of the substitution of serfs on feudal domains for the free peasantry and small landowners of the fourth century,[4]—although I suspect that

[1] P. Ross.-Georg. 6, 9 (Peter Jernstedt, *Die Kome-Aphrodito Papyri der Sammlung Lichacov*, in Gregor Zereteli *Papyri Russischer und Georgischer Sammlungen*, vol. iv, Tiflis, 1927.

[2] P. Lond. 1345. Bell properly translated "persons of distinction," although the attempt in Preisigke (*s. v.*) to interpret differently was natural until another case of this meaning was known.

[3] P. Lond. 1529.

[4] *Cf.* Gelzer *Studien*, iii.

the freedom of the earlier period and the sad conditions of the sixth century are both capable of exaggeration. Schnebel's comment on the situation at the Hermopolis estate is a suitable summary of at least one piece of evidence:

While papyri already published have revealed to us much that is ugly about the great nobles of the period of decline, we can assert, on the other side, that the *comites* of our document managed their estate with great wisdom and great humanity. They spent a great part of their revenues in improvements (even the expenses for irrigation must partly be claimed as such) and in one year, when an accident of nature severely damaged the produce of their estates, they remitted to their stricken tenants 30.72-100%, usually 33%, of their liabilities, although themselves allowed by the state no tax alleviation whatever in consequence.[1]

But perhaps one reservation should be made before we speak about the period of decline. Rostovtzeff refers to two opposite tendencies in agrarian policy in Greco-Roman Egypt, a policy of encouraging individual initiative and a policy of enforcing government control.[2] In the Byzantine period Egypt at last was not directed by government policies but began to live its own national and social life and let the government adapt itself as best it could. It is interesting to speculate what might have happened in another century. Would feudalism and nationalism have developed further, and how would the Coptic church have related itself to the nobles? But we shall never know.

[1] Schnebel, "Agricultural Ledger," p. 45.

[2] Rostowzew, *Studien*.

# BIBLIOGRAPHY

## I. Papyri and Inscriptions


BGU, *Aegyptische Urkunden aus den Königlichen Museen zu Berlin.* Berlin (Weidmann), 1895-1926, 7 vols.

"Greek-Coptic Glossary." H. I. Bell and W. E. Crum, "A Greek-Coptic Glossary" in *Aegyptus,* vol. vi, Milan, 1925, pp. 177-226.

Ostraca, Ulrich Wilcken, *Griechische Ostraka aus Aegypten und Nubien,* Leipzig (Giesecke and Devrient), 1899, 2 vols.

P. Amherst, Bernard P. Grenfell, Arthur S. Hunt, *The Amherst Papyri,* London (Oxford University Press), 1900-1901, 2 vols.

P. Baden, Friedrich Bilabel, *Griechische Papyri (Veröffentlichungen aus den badischen Papyrus-Sammlungen,* hft. 4), Heidelberg, 1924, 180 pp.

P. Basel, E. Rabel, and others, *Papyrusurkunden der öffentlichen Bibliothek der Universität zu Basel (Abhandlungen der Königlichen Gesellschaft der Wissenschaften zu Göttingen,* Philologisch-Historische Klasse, N. F. XVI, 3), Berlin (Weidmann), 1917, 100 pp.

P. Berlin Möller, Sigurd Möller, *Griechische Papyri aus dem Berliner Museum,* Gothenberg (Elander), 1929, viii-95 pp.

P. Cairo, Jean Maspero, *Papyrus grecs d'époque byzantine (Catalogue général des antiquités égyptiennes du musée du Caire),* Cairo (Institut français d'archéologie orientale), 1911-1916, 3 vols.

P. Cairo Zenon, C. C. Edgar, *Zenon Papyri (Catalogue général des antiquités égyptiennes du musée du Caire),* Cairo (Institut français d'archéologie orientale), 1925-1928, 3 vols.

P. Flor., Girolamo Vitelli, Domenico Comparetti, *Papiri Fiorentini* (Domenico Comparetti and Girolamo Vitelli, *Papiri Grecoegizii*), Milan (Hoepli), 1906-1915, 3 vols.

P. Giessen, Ernst Kornemann, Paul M. Meyer, *Griechische Papyri im Museum der oberhessichen Geschichtsvereins zu Giessen,* Leipzig (Teubner), 1910-1912, xiii-91-104-168 pp.

P. Grenfell II, Bernard P. Grenfell, Arthur S. Hunt, *New Classical Fragments and other Greek and Latin Papyri (Greek Papyri, Series II),* Oxford (Clarendon Press), 1897, xii-217 pp.

P. Hamburg, Paul M. Meyer, *Griechische Papyrusurkunden der Hamburger Staats-und Universitätsbibliothek,* Leipzig (Teubner), 1924, vol. i, 269 pp.

P. Iand., C. Kalbfleisch, and others, *Papyri Iandanae*, Leipzig (Teubner), 1912-1914, 4 fasc.

P. Klein. Form., C. Wessely, *Griechische Papyrusurkunden kleineren Formats* (C. Wessely, ed., *Studien zur Palaeographie und Papyruskunde*, vols. iii and viii), Leipzig (Avenar), 1904-1908, 2 vols.

P. Leipzig, Ludwig Mitteis, *Griechische Urkunden der Papyrussammlung zu Leipzig*, Leipzig (Teubner), 1906, xii, 380 pp.

P. Lond., F. G. Kenyon, H. I. Bell, *Greek Papyri in the British Museum*, London (British Museum), 1893-1917, 5 vols.

P. Munich, August Heisenberg, Leopold Wenger, *Byzantinische Papyri in der Königlichen Hof-und Staatsbibliothek zu München*, Leipzig (Teubner), 1914 (ix), 203 pp.

P. Ox., Bernard P. Grenfell, Arthur S. Hunt, H. Idris Bell, *The Oxyrhynchus Papyri*, London (Egypt Exploration Fund), 1898-1927, xvii vols.

P. Rainer, Jakob Kroll, *Corpus Papyrorum Raineri*, vol. ii, *Koptische Texte*, Vienna (K. K. Hof-und Staatsdruckerei), 1895, viii, 225 pp.

P. Ross.-Georg., Peter Jernstedt, *Die Kome-Aphrodito Papyri der Sammlung Lichacov* (Gregor Zereteli, ed., *Papyri Russischer und Georgischer Sammlungen*, vol. ii), Tiflis (University), 1927, viii, 130 pp.

P. Ryl., Arthur S. Hunt, *Catalogue of the Greek Papyri in the John Rylands Library, Manchester*, Manchester (University Press), 1911-1915, 2 vols.

PSI, G. Vitelli, *Papiri Greci e Latini* (*Pubblicazioni della societá italiana per la ricerca dei papiri greci e latini in Egitto*), Florence (Ariani), 1912-1929, 9 vols.

P. Strassburg, Friedrich Preisigke, *Griechische Papyrus der kaiserlichen Universitäts-und Landesbibliothek zu Strassburg*, Leipzig (Hinrichs), 1912-1920, 2 vols.

P. Stud. Pal. X, Carl Wessely, *Griechische Texte zur Topographie Ägyptens* (Carl Wessely, ed., *Studien zur Palaeographie und Papyruskunde*, vol. x), Leipzig (Avenar), 1910 (iv)-183 pp.

P. Stud. Pal. XX, Carl Wessely, *Textus Graeci* papyrorum qui in libro "Papyrus Erzherzog Rainer-Führer durch die Ausstellung Wien, 1894" descripti sunt (Carl Wessely, ed., *Studien zur Palaeographie und Papyruskunde*, vol. xx), Leipzig (Haessel), 1921 (iv)-163 pp.

Rec. Chrét., Gustave Lefebvre, *Recueil des inscriptions grecques chrétiennes d'Égypte*, Cairo (Institut français d'archéologie orientale), 1907, xl, 173 pp., and "Égypte chrétienne, iv, Inscriptions coptes et grecques" in *Annales du service des antiquités de l'Égypte*, vol. xi, 1911, pp. 238-250.

### II. Literary and Legal Sources

——, *Chronicon Paschale* (J. P. Migne, ed., *Patrologia Graeca,* vol. 92, Paris, 1865, cols. 70-1028).

(C. T.), *Theodosiani Libri XVI* (ed. Th. Mommsen), Berlin (Weidmann), 1905, 2 vols.

——, *Corpus Iuris Civilis,* Berlin (Weidmann), 3 vols.

(C. J.), vol. ii, " Codex Iustinianus " (ed. P. Krueger), 9th ed., 1915.

(Nov., Edicts), vol. iii, Novellae (R. Schoell and W. Kroll, ed.), 4th ed., 1920.

Innocent of Maronia, Letter in J. D. Mansi, ed., *Sacrorum Conciliorum Nova et Amplissima Collectio,* vol. viii, Florence, 1762, cols. 817-834.

John of Nikiou, *Chronicle* (M. H. Zotenberg, *Chronique de Jean, évêque de Nikiou,* in *Notices et extraits des manuscrits de la bibliothèque nationale,* vol. 24, Paris, 1883, pp. 125-608).

Leontius of Neapolis, *Life of John the Almoner* (Heinrich Gelzer, ed., *Leontios' von Neopolis Leben des heiligen Iohannes des Barmherzigen, Erzbischofs von Alexandrien* (G. Krüger ed., *Sammlung ausgewählter kirchen-und dogmengeschichtlichen Quellenschriften,* hft. 5), Freiburg (Mohr), 1893, xlviii-202 pp.

John Malalas, *Chronographia* (J. P. Migne, ed., *Patrologia Graeca,* vol. 97, Paris, 1860, cols. 65-718).

Michael Syrus, *Chronicle* (J. B. Chabot, ed., *Chronique de Michel le Syrien,* Paris, 1901-1924, 4 vols.).

Procopius, *De Bello Persico* (J. Haury, ed., *Procopii Caesariensis Opera Omnia*), Leipzig (Teubner), 1905-1913, 3 vols.

Theophanes, *Chronographia* (J. P. Migne, *Patrologia Graeca,* vol. 108, Paris, 1863, cols. 55-1010).

### III. Modern Books and Articles

H. I. Bell, " The Byzantine Servile State in Egypt " in *The Journal of Egyptian Archaelogy,* vol. iv, London, 1917, pp. 86-106.

——, " The Decay of a Civilization " in *The Journal of Egyptian Archaelogy,* vol. x, London, 1924, pp. 207-216.

——, " An Epoch in the Agrarian History of Egypt " in *Recueil d'études égyptologiques dédiées a la mémoire de Jean-François Champollion* (*Bibliothèque de l'école des hautes études, sciences historiques et philologiques,* fasc. 234), Paris (Champion), 1922, iv-788 pp., pp. 261-271.

A. E. R. Boak, " The Master of the Offices in the Later Roman and Byzantine Empires " in A. E. R. Boak and James Dunlap, *Two Studies in Later Roman and Byzantine Administration,* New York (Macmillan), 1924, x-324 pp., pp. vii-160.

J. B. Bury, *History of the Later Roman Empire,* London (Macmillan), 1923, 2 vols.

Luigi Cantarelli, "La serie dei prefetti de Egitto: III Dalla morte di Teodosio I alla conquista araba," in *Atti della R. Accademia dei Lincei*, serie quinta, memorie della classa di scienze morali, storiche, e filologiche, vol. xiv, Rome, 1913, pp. 385-440.

Roth Clausing, *The Roman Colonate*, New York, 1925, 333 pp.

Richard Delbrueck, *Die Consulardiptychen und verwandte Denkmäler* (Richard Delbrueck and Hans Lietzmann, *Studien zur Spätantiken Kunstgeschichte*, 2), *Berlin* (De Gruyter), 1929, 2 vols.

Charles Diehl, "Une crise monetaire au VIe siècle" in *Revue des Études Grecques*, vol. 33, Paris, 1921, pp. 158-166.

Matthias Gelzer, "Altes und Neues aus der byzantinisch-ägyptischen Verwaltungsmisere' in *Archiv für Papyrusforschung*, vol. v, Leipzig 1913, pp. 346-377.

——, *Studien zur Byzantinischen Verwaltung Ägyptens* (*Leipziger Historische Abhandlungen*, hft. 13), Leipzig (Quelle and Meyer), 1909, 107 pp.

——, "Zum *αὐτόπρακτον σχῆμα* der P. Aphrodito Cairo" in *Archiv für Papyrusforschung*, vol. v, Leipzig, 1913, pp. 188-189.

Robert Grosse, *Römische Militärwesen von Gallienus bis zum Beginn der byzantinischen Themenverfassung*, Berlin (Weidmann), 1920, xvi-346 pp.

Edward Rochie Hardy, Jr., "New Light on the Persian Occupation of Egypt" in the *Journal of the Society of Oriental Research*, vol. xiii, New York, 1929, pp. 185-189.

Johannes Leipoldt, *Schenute von Atripe und die Entstehung des national ägyptischen Christentums* (O.v. Gebhardt and A. Harnack, *Texte und Untersuchungen zur Geschichte der altchristlichen Literatur*, vol. xxv, 1), Leipzig (Hinrichs), 1903, x-214 pp.

Willy Liebenam, *Fasti Consulares Imperii Romani* (Hans Lietzmann, ed., *Kleine Texte für Theologische Vorlesungen und Übungen*, 41-43), Bonn (Marcus and Weber), 1909, 128 pp.

Jean Maspero, "Un dernier poéte grec d'Égypte, Dioscore fils d'Apollos" in *Revue des Études Grecques*, vol. xxiv, Paris, 1911, pp. 426-481.

——, *Histoire de Patriarches d'Alexandrie depuis la morte de l'empéreur Anastase jusqu'a la reconciliation des églises Jacobites (518-616)*. (*Bibliothèque de l'école des hautes études, sciences historiques et philologiques*, fasc. 237), Paris (Champion), 1923, ix-429 pp.

——, *Organisation militaire de l'Égypt byzantine* (*Bibliothèque de l'école des hautes études, sciences historiques et philologiques*, fasc. 201), Paris (Champion), 1912, 158 pp.

——, "Les papyrus Beaugé" in *Bulletin de l'institut français d'ärchéologie orientale*, vol. x, Cairo, 1912, pp. 131-157.

J. Grafton Milne, "Egyptian Nationalism under Greek and Roman Rule" in *The Journal of Egyptian Archaeology*, vol. xiv, London, 1928, pp. 226-234.

——, *A History of Egypt Under Roman Rule* (Flinders Petrie, ed., *A History of Egypt*, vol. v), 3rd ed., London (Methuen) (1924), xxiv-331 pp.

——, "The Currency of Egypt in the Fifth Century" in the *Numismatic Chronicle*, series v, vol. vi, London, 1926, pp. 43-92.

——, "Feudal Currency in Roman Egypt" in *Ancient Egypt*, London, March, 1926, pp. 5-9.

Friedrich Preisigke, *Wörterbuch der griechischen Papyrusurkunden* (Emil Kiessling, ed.), vols. i-iii, Berlin, 1925-1929.

Theodor Reil, *Beiträge zur Kenntnis des Gewerbes im hellenistischen Ägypten*, Leipzig (Noske), 1913 (8)-212 pp.

M. Rostowzew, "Die Domänenpolizei in dem römischen Kaiserreiche" in *Philologus*, vol. 54 (N. F. vol. xviii), Leipzig, 1905, pp. 297-307.

——, *Studien zur Geschichte des römischen Kolonates* (*Archiv für Papyrusforschung*, Beiheft 1), Leipzig (Teubner), 1910, xii-432 pp.

Germaine Rouillard, *L'administration civile de l'Égypte byzantine*, 2nd ed., Paris (Geuthner), 1928, xvi-208 pp.

Michael Schnebel, "An Agricultural Ledger in P. Bad. 96" in *The Journal of Egyptian Archaeology*, vol. xiv, London, 1928, pp. 34-45.

——, *Die Landwirtschaft im hellenistischen Ägypten* (Leopold Wenger, ed. *Münchener Beiträge zur Papyrusforschung und antiken Rechtsgeschichte*, hft. 7), vol. i, Munich (Beck), 1925, xviii-379 pp.

Otto Seeck, *Die Briefe des Libanius* (O.v. Gebhardt and Adolf Harnack, *Texte und Untersuchungen zur Geschichte der altchristlichen Literatur*, vol. 30), Leipzig (Hinrichs), 1906 (vi)-496 pp.

Leopold Wenger, *Volk und Staat in Ägypten am Ausgang der Römerherrschaft*, Munich (Bayerische Akademie der Wissenschaften), 1922, 58 pp.

L. Mitteis and V. Wilcken, *Grundzüge und Chrestomathie der Papyruskunde*, Leipzig (Teubner), 1912, 4 vols.

Friedrich von Woess, *Das Asylwesen Ägyptens in der Ptolemäerzeit und die spätere Entwicklung* (Leopold Wenger, *Münchener Beitrage zur Papyrusforschung und antiken Rechtsgeschichte*, hft. 5), Munich (Beck), 1923, xii-282 pp.

Francis de Zulueta, *Patronage in the Later Empire* (in Paul Vinogradoff, *Oxford Studies in Social and Legal History*, vol. i, 2), Oxford (Clarendon Press), 1909, 78 pp.

# INDICES

## I. GREEK



## II. ENGLISH

## III. LIST OF DOCUMENTS OF WHICH THE DATE OR READING IS DISCUSSED

Bei Fragen zur Produktsicherheit wenden Sie sich bitte an:
If you have any questions regarding product safety, please contact:

Walter de Gruyter GmbH
Genthiner Straße 13
10785 Berlin
productsafety@degruyterbrill.com